Contents

D1380132

About the author

Toni Battison is a trained nurse who has had considerable practical and teaching experience during her career working with older people and carers, including that of District Nursing Sister, Health Promotion Advisor, Health Lecturer for a Certificate in Health Education course and as the manager of a small charity. She is now retired from the NHS and does some part-time freelance work in the field of health information. Toni has written many publications promoting good health and is a regular contributor to local radio. She is an Associate Member of the Guild of Health Writers.

Toni has always been concerned about the need to support carers and patients to enable them to get the best from local and national services, as she believes that people obtain great benefit from being able to help themselves. Whilst working for the Cambridge and Huntingdon Health Authority she helped create an information centre for patients and visitors at Addenbrooke's Hospital and, with other carers, started the Telephone Information Line for Carers of Elderly People, in the Cambridge area. She was joint winner of the Ian Nichol Prize for Health Promotion in 1990 and 1992 for these projects.

Toni lives near Cambridge with her husband and has three grown-up daughters. She is the main carer for her mother, who lives with her and is in her late 80s. In the past Toni helped her mother care for her father, following a series of strokes and epilepsy, until he died at home. Her experience in caring for her parents has given a personal perspective that complements her professional role.

Acknowledgements

The author thanks the many carers, friends and colleagues who contributed valuable help and advice towards the production of this book. In particular:

Joan Bragg, for sharing her feelings and memories about Peter's illness;

Val Beamish, State Registered Dietitian;

Dr Sarah Brewer, medical writer;

Jill Briggs, Lead Practitioner for District Nurses, and Sally Feast, Senior Occupational Therapist, both from Lifespan Healthcare NHS Trust;

Beryl Sarsfield, Carers' Support Worker, Cambridgeshire Social Services;

Debrae Walsh, Senior Lecturer/Aromatherapist, Homerton College, Cambridge, School of Health Studies;

Gill Westland, Psychotherapist, Cambridge Body Psychotherapy Centre;

A J Geddes, Bendall & Sons, Solicitors;

Dr S G P Webster, Consultant Physician, Addenbrooke's NHS Trust;

The staff and volunteers at Directions Plus, Cambridge.

In addition I thank all the national organisations that offer information and support to carers in the broadest sense, whose materials have helped to inform and influence my thinking, and to the people at Age Concern for their support and advice throughout the stages of publication, especially Richard Holloway, Vinnette Marshall and Ro Lyon.

Introduction

Coronary heart disease (CHD) is the most common form of heart disease. Most people know something about coronary heart disease, because a relative or friend is affected and because it is a topic of ill-health that is widely discussed in the media and society in general. Unfortunately, coronary heart disease is the greatest cause of disability and death throughout the western world today. CHD causes over 120,000 deaths a year in the UK: approximately one in four deaths in men and one in six deaths in women. Deaths from CHD are highest in Scotland and the North of England and lowest in the South of England. (The premature death rate for CHD for men living in Scotland is almost 50 per cent higher than in the South West of England and around 80 per cent higher for women.) Almost 2 million people in the UK are suffering from angina, which is the most common form of CHD.

These are difficult figures to grasp, and they make sombre reading if you are caring for someone who is suffering from a heart problem. The good news is that treatments and care nowadays are excellent; many people with heart problems are able to lead relatively normal lives; and the number of deaths linked to coronary heart disease have fallen in recent years. The outlook is optimistic; however, there are some serious concerns regarding the health of future generations because of current dietary habits and lifestyle changes. Coronary heart disease (and its associated risk factors) was one of the main conditions included in the government's health promotion programme *The Health of the Nation*, at the end of the 20th Century, which aimed to reduce the level of ill-health and death in a number of key areas. Targets included changes or reduction in factors such as diet and nutrition, obesity, smoking, blood pressure and alcohol consumption.

The purpose of this book is to offer information, advice and support to people who care for someone with coronary heart disease and the associated problems of the circulatory system, and to provide an insight into some of the issues related to caring. Throughout the text there are quotes from people with heart disease and their carers and from health professionals; the names have been changed but they are real people. The person you are caring for may be a spouse, a relative or a friend but, for simplicity, they are referred to always as 'your relative'.

The 2001 Census found that there are about six million carers in the UK. However, this is generally accepted to be an underestimate – the true figure is probably 10 million people (including children who fulfil the main caring role). In simple terms, this means that approximately one in ten people is looking after someone who, because of ill-health or old age, can no longer maintain complete independence. The issues are no longer hidden, and the value to society of these 'informal carers' is slowly being recognised. Acts of Parliament have been passed that create a firm base for pursuing the rights and needs of both carers and the people they are caring for.

Carers are beginning to seek assistance but surveys carried out by Carers UK continue to find that many people do not know that they are entitled to services and support. The financial costs of caring can be significant. One Carers UK survey concluded that 77 per cent of people questioned were worse off financially as a result of becoming carers.

Carers UK

'These issues must be addressed if we are to make the best use of the most precious of all resources in community care – the unpaid help, willingly given, of carers.'

(Source: *Still Battling?* 1997)

This book outlines what is available for carers through statutory and voluntary organisations, and provides an introduction to a number of techniques and complementary therapies that will help you to cope with the caring situation. Unfortunately, there are shortfalls and gaps in most local authority and health services, and there are rarely answers and solutions to every question and problem. Nevertheless, there are sources of support to help you cope with the hard work, the stress and the feelings of frustration, and enough information is available to make finding your way around the caring maze less difficult.

1 What do we mean by heart disease?

Heart disease, in everyday terms, means any problem that affects both the heart and the circulation. The most common illness, coronary heart disease (CHD), is recognised as the biggest cause of disability and death in the western world. Coronary heart disease is not a single illness affecting the heart itself, but is a term used to describe problems that occur in the arteries immediately surrounding the heart. The coronary arteries supply the heart with oxygen-rich blood. When these become narrowed or blocked, the lack of blood may cause the pain of angina. Complete blockage means that part of the heart muscle dies for lack of blood; this is a heart attack.

The person you care for may already have had a heart attack, or they may have angina or another less common problem affecting their heart or circulatory system. This chapter describes these problems in greater detail, starting with the structure of the heart and the circulatory system. Knowing how the heart works will help you and your relative to understand what has gone wrong, and why some of the tests and treatments are necessary. As a result, you will both feel more confident about asking questions, which could help to make visits to the hospital or doctor less distressing and less frequent.

The chapter also looks at some of the risk factors affecting other family members and offers some advice from a doctor and a carer about recovery after a major heart attack.

The structure and function of the heart

How does it work?

The heart is a bag of muscle about the size of a clenched fist that acts as two separate but interrelated pumps. It is divided into four sections (chambers), each separated by a strong dividing wall. The central wall between the left and right halves is normally unbroken, whilst the wall dividing the top chambers (atria) from the bottom chambers (ventricles) contains a one-way opening (valve) to allow the blood to pass through (see Figure 1 overleaf). Each chamber is about the same size but the walls of the ventricles are much thicker than those of the atria because they have to work harder pumping blood away from the heart. The atria have less work to do because their function is to receive blood from the veins into the heart and pump it down to the ventricles. The valves stop the blood being pushed back in the wrong direction and can be one of the parts of the heart that become diseased and fail (valvular heart disease is described on pages 24–25).

The blood is carried through the body by arteries and veins. Each pumping action of the heart is triggered by an electrical impulse that sets off a sequence of events making up one heartbeat: first the atria contract, then the ventricles, followed by a resting phase.

How does the blood flow?

Think of a heart as being like the pump in a central heating system: water cannot get to the furthest radiator unless it is pushed there. The main function of the heart is to pump blood rich in oxygen to the muscles and organs all over the body. To do this the right atrium receives exhausted (de-oxygenated) blood, which is immediately pumped to the ventricle below. From here the strong muscle walls pump the de-oxygenated blood to the lungs where waste gas (carbon dioxide) is exchanged through the walls of the fine blood vessels for fresh oxygen. The newly oxygenated blood is carried directly back to the left side of the heart where the same pumping process pushes it to the extremities of the body. Oxygen, carried via the red blood cells, is then released along the way, bringing vital energy to every living tissue in the body. This demand for energy is constant but variable according to how active you are; for example, the need is much lower when you are asleep than when walking up a hill.

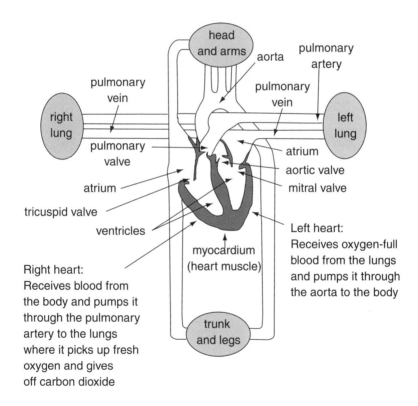

Figure 1 Diagram of the structure of the heart *(Redrawn by permission of the British Heart Foundation)*

Just as water pipes in the central heating system may get blocked with lime deposits, so may the arteries become narrowed or blocked with fatty deposits. The narrower the arteries, the less room there is for blood to flow. When a person is suffering from coronary heart disease, the blood supply to the heart is poor. This means there is insufficient oxygen to meet the increased demands on the heart during exercise; this causes the pain of angina.

Fact Box

- An average heart beats 70 times per minute, or 100,000 times per day.
- An average heart pumps 80ml of blood with each beat, or 8,000 litres per day.
- A heart valve opens and closes about 40 million times a year.
- About 20 per cent of adults in the UK have high blood pressure.
- Nearly 2 million people in the UK suffer from angina each year.
- Over 270,000 people in the UK have a heart attack each year.
- Around 28,500 people have coronary bypass operations in the UK each year.
- Over 378,000 inpatient cases are treated for coronary heart disease in NHS hospitals each year.

(Sources: first four entries: *Beating Heart Disease the Natural Way* by Dr Sarah Brewer; final four entries: British Heart Foundation Statistics Database 2003.)

What are the risk factors?

Fiona, a doctor

'Family history cannot be changed, but otherwise the risks of heart disease can be reduced.'

The chances of developing coronary heart disease will depend on a range of contributing circumstances, which are known as 'risk factors'.

The rate at which it gets worse also depends on these factors. The risk factors linked to coronary heart disease are:

- family history of heart disease;
- smoking cigarettes;
- increasing age;
- untreated high blood pressure;
- diet high in saturated (animal) fat;
- abnormally high levels of blood fats (eg cholesterol);
- being overweight or obese;
- taking insufficient exercise;
- drinking large amounts of alcohol;
- being male – until middle age; then the risk rate for post-menopausal women equals that for men; and
- having diabetes that cannot easily be controlled.

Although the ageing process cannot be slowed down and family history cannot be altered, many of the other factors can be changed to improve general health and reduce the future risk of heart disease. Chapter 3 offers ideas and suggestions to help you make improvements in lifestyle.

Eric, a doctor

'It's never too late to improve your lifestyle.'

What can go wrong?

High blood pressure (hypertension)

High blood pressure affects about 10–20 per cent of the adult population but, unfortunately, remains undiagnosed in many people until a more serious illness requires medical attention. Although it is the forerunner of many heart attacks or strokes, it rarely causes symptoms even when dangerously high.

When the pressure of blood is measured (BP: blood pressure) the reading is affected by several elements: the volume of blood and its stickiness (viscosity); the strength of the heart's contraction (pushing the blood along); the rate of the beat; and the diameter, elasticity and resistance of the arterial walls. It is entirely normal for blood pressure to be raised after physical activity and to differ throughout the day but a person with hypertension will have blood pressure readings that are high even at rest. Hypertension is more common in men than in women and tends to increase during middle age.

Blood pressure is usually measured on the arteries of the arm by inflating a special cuff that is wrapped round the upper arm. The cuff is attached to an instrument that gives a reading of two numbers: the higher number (systolic pressure) relates to the pressure in the circulation as the heart contracts and pushes blood into the aorta; the lower number (diastolic pressure) indicates the pressure in the system as the heart relaxes between beats. The average reading for a healthy young adult is 120/80 while at rest, but a person in middle age could register a pressure of 150/90. It is likely that medical treatment would be started if the blood pressure regularly exceeded 160/95.

The risk of raised blood pressure is commonly linked with factors that can also cause coronary heart disease (such as obesity, a family history, lack of exercise, smoking cigarettes and high consumption of alcohol). In particular, it is thought to be directly related to the total amount of salt in the diet. Reducing their intake of salt to lower the systolic blood pressure could also help to reduce the risk of stroke or coronary heart disease for many people.

High blood pressure puts extra strain on the arterial wall linings and speeds up the development of atherosclerosis (see below). In a small number of people, raised blood pressure is caused by an illness, such as kidney disease, and will be treated accordingly.

Management of hypertension

Regular health checks are one way of keeping abreast of potential problems. Although repeated checks are needed to make an accurate diagnosis, do be realistic about how often these are sought, as a phenomenon known as 'white-coat hypertension' causes some people to become overanxious, leading to very frequent and unnecessary checks. If there are some concerns about the blood pressure rate, lifestyle changes would initially be recommended for people with a rate of 140/85. Such changes are often sufficient to lower the rate, but drug therapy would be considered if the changes did not lower the level satisfactorily, followed by regular monitoring and review.

Atherosclerosis

'Atherosclerosis' is the medical term used to describe the problem caused by 'furring up' of the arteries. It starts at an early age, and several factors contribute to the slow, thickening process that in many people leads to angina and possibly a heart attack. At first, general wear and tear occurs, and so the artery walls become less smooth. Then fatty materials (cholesterol), produced naturally by the body and also taken in through a high-fat diet, stick to the walls, leaving patchy, porridge-like deposits that narrow the passageway.

In some people damage to the arteries is made worse by:

■ chemicals in cigarette smoke;
■ high blood pressure;
■ a family tendency to produce excess cholesterol; or
■ diabetes.

Lack of exercise and stress also play a part and eventually the artery loses its elasticity and becomes more fibrous. This is known as 'hardening' of the arteries, a term commonly used to describe the state of the blood vessels.

Will the problem get worse?

Many long-term problems can result from atherosclerosis as it builds up slowly for many years, affecting all parts of the body. The most common are:

- chronic (long-term) high blood pressure;
- permanent damage to organs such as the kidneys;
- poor peripheral circulation, particularly in the legs; or
- gradual loss of brain cells, leading to vascular dementia.

One sign of a serious problem is often the pain of mild angina, because the fatty 'plaques' in the artery walls restrict the flow of blood to the heart. If the plaques crack or become roughened, a blood clot forms over the damaged tissue; this process is called thrombosis, and 'thrombus' is another word for 'clot'. This may block the coronary artery and starve part of the heart muscle of blood, causing a heart attack. If a piece of clot breaks off, it can float in the blood until it wedges in a narrow blood vessel. A travelling clot is called an 'embolus' and the process is 'embolism'. A clot from the leg can travel to the lungs, causing the dangerous condition of 'pulmonary embolism'. Thrombosis or embolism in the brain arteries causes a stroke. Thrombosis can occur elsewhere in the body. In the leg, thrombosis cases redness, pain and swelling.

Varicose veins

Varicose veins are veins that have become stretched and dilated (widened) out of proportion to the amount of blood they carry. Veins vary greatly in thickness in different people, and even in different parts of the same vein. Therefore dilation will depend on the structure of the vein wall and any damage to the surrounding tissue (after an injury for example). These blood vessels are subject to degenerative and inflammatory changes from the late teens onwards, and are prevalent in women, particularly during pregnancy. The most common sites to be affected are the inner side of the lower leg, knee and thigh, the lower end of the bowel (haemorrhoids, piles), and the testicles (varicocele).

It is estimated that about two-thirds of adults in the UK have varicose veins; some people are more prone than others, owing to a combination of genetic make-up and occupational risks. Jobs that require long periods of standing, with little opportunity for vigorous muscle action, put a great strain on the veins and fail to provide the pumping action necessary to exert the muscle contractions that push the blood back to the heart. After a vein has begun to dilate, its walls become weaker and have poorer valve control; so the weight of blood pressing down in the veins increases and the symptoms worsen to the point that surrounding veins become affected as they take on a greater workload.

Symptoms of varicose veins are:

- bulging, 'knotted' veins at the surface of the legs (or other affected area of the body);
- fatigue on exertion;
- aching, particularly after standing; and
- swelling of the ankles.

Complications can occur that may need immediate or long-term treatment. If the area surrounding the vein becomes red, inflamed and painful (thrombophlebitis), it is important to seek urgent medical advice, because a blood clot can easily form and cause a blockage in the vein. The clot could then become infected or parts might break away and become lodged elsewhere in a critical area of the body. In the long term it is important to prevent breakdown of the surrounding skin, because the resulting varicose ulcer can be difficult to treat.

Treatment of varicose veins

Treatment will depend on the nature and severity of the problem. Inflammation of the vein and surrounding tissues may require immediate antibiotic drugs. The doctor may then prescribe support stockings; an injection into the vein to shrink and close the affected area; or surgical removal of the diseased veins. A number of self-help strategies are worth trying to ease the symptoms:

- If it is necessary to stand for long periods, keep the leg and calf muscles moving.
- If it is necessary to sit for long periods, keep the leg and calf muscles moving or get up and walk around.
- Lie down and rest when possible with the legs raised above heart level.
- Don't become overweight; or reduce weight levels if already overweight.

■ Don't become constipated, as this increases pressure on the abdominal and rectal veins, reducing their capacity to take blood flow away from the lower half of the body.

Peripheral vascular disease

Peripheral vascular disease occurs as a direct result of the 'hardening' and 'furring up' of the arteries, and causes unpleasant leg cramps when increased activity calls for additional oxygen to the muscles (see page 65). When the blood supply is reduced, exercise will cause severe pain, which stops at rest – a condition known as 'intermittent claudication'. If the blood supply is very poor, the pain can occur even when the person is resting. If your relative complains of painful leg cramps, be sure that the doctor is aware of this because high blood pressure and diabetes are known causes. People with severe peripheral vascular disease are at risk of developing leg ulcers, so take care to prevent skin damage from broken toenails or from knocking against furniture.

Treatment of peripheral vascular disease

Treatment may include:

■ exercise and maintaining activity levels;
■ stopping aggravation factors (such as smoking);
■ medication;
■ surgical bypass; or
■ surgical stretching of the artery at the site of the blockage.

Angina

Joan

'Peter suffered from angina. It wasn't too bad at first, affecting him only in cold weather, but even this made a difference to our lives – we became limited in what we could do as a couple. I didn't want to do things alone.'

Angina is the name given to pain or 'tightness' that starts in the chest and spreads upwards and outwards, affecting mainly the left side of the upper body. It is most painful in the neck, the jaw and down the left arm. The symptoms can vary in severity from temporary discomfort to a severe, crushing pain that makes the person feel breathless and sick. It occurs when the condition atherosclerosis (described on page 7) prevents sufficient oxygen reaching the heart muscle. The shortage of oxygen is felt when the heart is asked to work harder, and is most likely to occur during:

- increased activity or exertion;
- anxiety and emotional stress;
- exposure to cold and/or strong wind; or
- digestion of a heavy meal, when the blood supply is naturally diverted to the stomach.

Occasionally, people experience angina when resting or asleep. Doctors believe this is caused by a spasm (contraction) in the coronary artery that worsens the already poor blood supply. This type of angina is more unstable because the attacks of pain tend to vary in intensity and duration; it should never be ignored.

Fiona, a doctor

'If you are worried, worry the GP!'

The first signs of angina-like pain should always be investigated by a doctor, particularly if the feelings of tightness and breathlessness are relieved by resting. Many people treat the early symptoms as indigestion and delay visiting their doctor. It is better to seek early help and reassurance than to try to 'self-medicate' and allow the disease to progress to a stage where surgery may be necessary or, worse, a heart attack occurs. If the symptoms are severe, regard the condition as an emergency. Dial 999 for immediate help, as paramedical teams are trained to give treatment on the spot. The person who is ill should never attempt to drive to hospital. Angina is not a heart attack but it may be a warning sign that the person is at risk of having one.

11

Joan

'I was always aware of the angina and wondered if it would play up. It was always at the back of my mind.'

Diagnosis of angina

The doctor will make a diagnosis of angina based on a number of factors:

- the symptoms describing the pain: what it feels like, how long it lasts, when and how often it occurs;
- a review of the person's medical history, including any family history;
- a physical examination to check heartbeat and chest sounds; and
- various tests.

The tests (see page 15) are carried out to help the doctor understand the state of the heart and surrounding arteries. They will also rule out conditions with similar signs and symptoms that cause pains in the chest (such as problems in the digestive system or severe anxiety).

Eric, a doctor

'If someone is slowing down, has a pain or is more breathless, don't assume it's their age – seek advice from a GP.'

Treatment of angina

The treatment given will depend on the severity of the angina, and may need to be reviewed if the condition of the heart and surrounding arteries changes. The GP and hospital clinic will check the situation as often as is necessary. The two main courses of treatment are medication and surgery. To be effective, each will need to be supported by changes in general lifestyle and some adjustments may have to be made. Recovery rates are good and having angina should not stop your relative from living a full and active life. Chapter 3 deals more fully with ways to reduce the risk factors and thus help to prevent further attacks.

Joan

'It did affect Peter in some ways because he got frustrated. I would tell him not to fuss about things that would probably sort themselves out. He changed his hobbies a bit and did more indoors and less in the garden.'

Heart attack

The medical term for a heart attack is 'myocardial infarction', meaning damage to an organ (in this case the heart) caused by an interruption of the blood supply. Another term commonly used is 'coronary thrombosis', which takes its name from the action that occurs – a blockage to the blood supply of the heart caused by a blood clot lodged in a coronary artery. The severity of a heart attack depends on how much and where the heart muscle is affected. Damage to the conducting system may mean that the heartbeat cannot be co-ordinated; the heart is then unable to work properly, and may stop, causing sudden death. Very severe damage to large amounts of heart muscle may also be fatal.

The long-term build-up of arterial deposits, which can lead to a heart attack, are described in the sections on atherosclerosis (pages 7–8) and angina (pages 10–12). A heart attack can happen at any time, whether the person is resting or highly active.

Recognising a heart attack

A heart attack is a serious medical emergency, so never delay in calling an ambulance. A single tablet of aspirin is a useful immediate treatment that can be given at home, provided that the person is conscious and is able to swallow without difficulty. If the following symptoms are present, dial 999:

- pain – crushing, squeezing, pressing – starting in the central chest and radiating outward into the neck, shoulders and arms; unlike angina it does not ease with rest;
- paleness with cold sweats;
- breathlessness;

- palpitations (unusually rapid and strong heartbeat);
- nausea and vomiting;
- faintness or impaired consciousness.

Paramedical ambulance teams are trained to give excellent care for a suspected heart attack and will start emergency treatment before your relative reaches hospital. Make your relative lie down, and stay with them for reassurance and to check their condition. If they stop breathing, give mouth-to-mouth resuscitation. Cardiac massage should be given only by a person trained in the technique.

Fiona, a doctor

'The sooner the diagnosis of the heart attack is made, the better – the sooner treatment is started, the more likely it is to be effective.'

Diagnosis and hospital care

Someone with a suspected heart attack will be taken either directly to a coronary care unit (CCU) or to an accident and emergency (A&E) centre, depending on bed space and hospital facilities. Initially, a diagnosis is made from a description of the pain; tests (see page 15) are made at a later stage to confirm the preliminary diagnosis and the extent of damage to the heart muscle. Immediate treatment will include:

- various drugs (usually given through a vein in the arm) to relieve pain, dissolve the blood clot, regulate the heartbeat and bring about sedation;
- oxygen to help breathing;
- connection to an ECG (electrocardiograph) machine to monitor the heart's electrical waves;
- blood tests to detect changes in body chemistry; and
- initial bed rest, leading to gradually increased activity.

The care of patients differs according to their individual needs and the practice favoured by different consultants but all treatment works towards early mobility and discharge from hospital. Chapter 3 deals more fully with changes in lifestyle that may be necessary after a heart attack.

Inflammation of the heart

Inflammation or an infection in various parts of the heart is less common nowadays because treatments, particularly antibiotics and steroids, are readily available. The three main conditions are:

- **Endocarditis** – literally, an infection of the heart lining, including the *heart valves*. It usually occurs in valves that are already abnormal. People who know that they have damaged (or replacement) heart valves are advised to take special care with dental hygiene.
- **Myocarditis** – an infection of the *heart muscle*, which can develop after a severe attack of a viral illness with flu-like symptoms. Fortunately, this condition is very rare.
- **Pericarditis** – an infection of the *covering of the heart*, which can become inflamed after a heart attack or through a viral infection, causing pain and a general feeling of being unwell. As with myocarditis, the condition is rare.

What tests and treatments are given?

Diagnostic tests for heart conditions

The tests described here are the main ones used to inform doctors about the state of the heart and circulatory system, to help make a diagnosis and to decide upon appropriate treatment.

- **Electrocardiogram (ECG)** Small electrodes are attached to several points on the body to record any abnormalities in the electrical impulses of the heart. (The test is completely painless.) Patients who have had a heart attack have their ECG monitored continuously in the early stages. (Continuous monitoring is usually with a TV-style screen monitor rather than a paper recording.) The readings help to assess the amount of muscle damage and the exact area where it occurred.

■ **Blood tests** These are done to detect abnormal levels of body chemicals in the blood, indicating that a heart attack has taken place. The levels of enzymes (chemicals released by dead heart muscle) can be used to gauge the amount of damage.

■ **Angiocardiography** This technique is used when a more detailed picture of the heart and coronary arteries is necessary, for example before heart surgery. Liquid that shows up on X-ray is injected into the circulation, and outlines the coronary arteries as it flows through them. This can be seen on a screen monitor, and narrowing or blockage by atheroma or clot can be identified.

■ **Doppler ultrasound** This test uses high-frequency sound waves to determine the speed and direction of blood as it flows through the heart and circulatory system.

Eric, a doctor

'If you don't understand about any treatment, ask – again and again, if necessary.'

Medication (drugs) to treat heart conditions

The information given here is intended only as a brief outline of the main medicines used to treat different heart problems, so that you and your relative understand why medication is so important and what effects it can have. It can be confusing for a lay person but the words 'drug' and 'medicine' mean the same thing in medical terms. Some drugs must be taken regularly to prevent a condition getting worse (such as the long-term use of anticoagulants to 'thin' the blood), whereas others are taken only when symptoms develop, such as the pain of angina. It is important to check the information given on the label, and never stop using a drug without medical advice. If you are unsure about any aspect of medication your relative is taking, it's best to check with their own doctor or ask the local pharmacist.

Although there seem to be many drugs in use for the treatment of heart disease, in reality there are only a few main groups (described below). There are two main reasons for this abundance of drugs:

- Any one drug may be available in several variations, which enables doctors to prescribe the best 'match' for the person's symptoms; it may take several attempts to find the one that gives the best results with the least side (unwanted) effects.
- Different manufacturers give the same basic drug a different colour and trade name. Think of medicine like coffee on a supermarket shelf – the names and the packaging are different but the granules are the same.

How do drugs get into the system?

There are three main ways to give drugs. The most common route is through the mouth, as tablets, capsules or liquid; some drugs work better by being injected into the bloodstream; and occasionally they are given via the skin. The various methods are:

- **Aerosol** The drug is sprayed directly onto or under the tongue, where it will be absorbed quickly.
- **Buccal** The tablet is placed between the upper lip and gum, and is a much slower method of absorption (four to six hours).
- **Intramuscular** An injection is given deep into a muscle, usually the buttock or thigh.
- **Intravenous** The liquid drug is injected into a vein, rapidly by syringe or slowly by a drip feed. Drugs are given this way to dissolve blood clots in the case of a suspected heart attack.
- **Self-adhesive patches** This method, which gives a slow absorption of the drug, is sometimes used in the prevention of angina.
- **Subcutaneous** An injection is made just under the surface of the skin. The anticoagulant drug heparin is sometimes given by this method.
- **Sublingual** A tablet is placed under the tongue where it dissolves and is absorbed quickly into the bloodstream, going directly to the heart without being destroyed by the liver first. This method is used for easing the pain of angina, and means that the drug can easily be taken without liquid. However, it has now largely been superseded by the aerosol spray method.

The main drugs used in the treatment of heart problems fall into several groups; some people need a combination of medication to produce the best results.

Drug treatments for angina

Nitrates (eg glyceryl trinitrate: GTN) are used very effectively in the treatment of angina. They relax the walls of arteries and veins to allow an increased flow of blood and reduce the amount of work the heart has to do. Side effects can include headaches, dizziness or 'flushing' of the face.

Beta blockers (eg propranolol) are used to slow down and lower the force of the heartbeat. They are particularly good during exercise and in times of stress, because they block the passage of hormones such as adrenaline that stimulate the nervous system, making the heart work harder. Side effects can include tiredness, fatigue, cold and tingling in the hands and feet and, occasionally, nausea and diarrhoea, skin rashes or nightmares. They are not suitable for people with asthma, as they may bring on an attack.

Calcium channel blockers (eg nifedipine) act in a more complicated way. Calcium is a mineral essential for the work of all body cells connected with muscle contraction. These drugs block the level of calcium entering a cell and help to control the strength of the contraction and relax the muscle wall. This in turn increases the blood supply and reduces the work of the heart. Side effects can include headaches, arrhythmia (abnormal heart rhythm), swollen ankles or 'flushing' of the face.

Potassium channel activators (eg nicorandil) are new drugs. They work mainly by dilating (widening) the artery walls to increase blood supply to the heart muscle and by triggering a natural process that allows heart cells a brief rest when they are lacking in oxygen. This last action can prevent cells dying from shortage of oxygen, thus reducing the risks of angina and heart attack. Side effects can include headaches, 'flushing', indigestion or dizziness.

Drug treatments for high blood pressure

Diuretics (eg bendrofluazide) are also known as 'water tablets' and are used mainly to reduce the amount of fluid and salt in the body; this in turn lowers blood pressure and subsequently the work of the heart. They may also help to dilate small arteries. Some diuretics cause too much potassium to be lost from the body. This can be harmful, so a potassium supplement or a change of drug may be needed to correct the problem. Side effects can include weakness, dizziness, faintness, nausea or vomiting, and are linked to an increased risk of developing gout if uric acid levels in the blood are raised. Certain diuretics can affect blood sugar control, so this type (thiazide) should not be taken by anyone with diabetes. People who take diuretics should be careful about the amount of salt in their diet because this can counteract their effects; a dietitian or the practice nurse can give advice about this.

ACE (angiotensin-converting enzyme) inhibitors (eg enalapril) are used to reduce the production of the angiotensin-converting enzyme (a chemical), which constricts blood vessels. When combined with a diuretic, these drugs increase the blood supply to the kidneys and help the flow of urine, although this can act in reverse if the kidneys are already diseased. ACE inhibitors are generally well tolerated by most users. Side effects can include a cough, dizziness, skin rash or impaired taste; however, improved versions of these drugs usually cause fewer problems.

Angiotensin II antagonists (eg losartan) act in a similar way to ACE inhibitors but can be used as an alternative for people who develop a cough when taking an ACE inhibitor.

Alpha blockers (eg prazosin) act to reduce blood pressure by dilating arteries and veins. They are used if the drugs mentioned above are not successful alone. Side effects can include too great a fall in blood pressure (especially after the first dose), tiredness, dizziness or weakness.

Beta blockers and calcium channel blockers (discussed on page 18).

Drug treatments for dissolving and preventing blood clots (thrombolytic drugs or 'clotbusters')

Streptokinase is used only in an emergency for quick intravenous action after a heart attack, to break up a clot. It is not used if there is a risk of bleeding from other parts of the body, for example soon after an operation.

Heparin is an anticoagulant, used to prevent further clotting taking place. It is given urgently by intravenous injection; or a newer form may be given subcutaneously (under the skin) over a longer period.

Warfarin is given by mouth as a long-term anticoagulant to prevent clots forming. It is commonly used for people who have valvular heart disease, especially those who have been given a replacement heart valve. Warfarin is also used to treat deep-vein thrombosis (clots in the veins of the legs), to help prevent blood clots moving to the lungs. People who take anticoagulants should always carry an identification card because of the increased risk of internal bleeding. The doctor or pharmacist should always be told that your relative is taking an anticoagulant if other treatment is being prescribed. The action of anticoagulants can be affected by many other drugs, including antibiotics and aspirin.

Aspirin has fairly recently been recognised as an effective treatment in the prevention of blood clots and is now widely used for people who have coronary heart disease or who have had a stroke. However, it is not wise for healthy people to take aspirin as a long-term precaution, because it can cause digestive problems and occasionally triggers asthmatic attacks.

Drug treatments for abnormal rhythm of the heart and heart failure

Several groups of drugs are used to regulate and control disturbances in the normal heartbeat, often in a combination to produce the best effect. They work by making the beat stronger or by reducing resistance in the arteries.

Arrhythmics (eg amiodarone) are used when the heart rhythm is seriously erratic. Their use must be monitored carefully because they frequently give unpleasant side effects, including headaches, 'flushing' of the face, dizziness or stomach disorders. In some people they may adversely affect the lungs, liver, skin colour or thyroid gland.

Beta blockers and calcium channel blockers (discussed on page 18).

Digoxin is the main drug used to slow the heart when it is beating fast and irregularly (atrial fibrillation). It is especially useful when the heart is struggling to function in this abnormal rhythm, as the drug strengthens the heart's contraction as well as slowing its rate. The main side effects are loss of appetite, vomiting and disturbance of heart rhythm. It may be necessary to do blood tests to measure the amount of digoxin in the person's blood to make sure that the dose is just right.

Drug treatments for lowering cholesterol

High levels of cholesterol are treated first by adjusting the amount eaten in the diet (see Chapter 3). The second method, treatment by drugs, is used if the levels remain high after dietary changes and the person is at risk from coronary heart disease. There are several types of drugs commonly used to lower blood cholesterol levels.

Statins (eg simvastatin) are the main type of drugs used. They reduce cholesterol levels by slowing down its production in the liver. According to the British Heart Foundation's booklet *Reducing Your Blood Cholesterol*, statins can reduce total cholesterol levels by more than 20 per cent. Treating people in their 70s with statins is as effective as it is in middle-aged people. They must be taken for at least five years. Side effects can include discomfort in muscles that can be felt as non-cardiac chest pain, flatulence (wind), constipation and fatigue. Around 1.8 million people in the UK are on statins on the advice of doctors monitoring their condition. From July 2004 a low 10mg dose will be available at pharmacies without a prescription. The pills will be available to all men aged 55 and over, and to women and men aged 45 and over with known risk factors for heart disease. The low-dose drug is expected to cost about £15 a month. Statins will continue to be available on prescription, but the threshold is high: a 30 per cent chance of a heart attack in the next 10 years.

Resins (eg colestipol) are also called **'bile acid binding drugs'**. They work by stopping bile acids being re-absorbed into the gut. The liver responds by breaking down more cholesterol into bile acids, which are then passed out as waste products. Resins come in powder form. They are effective but can be unpleasant to take because large amounts of granules must be swallowed. Side effects can include digestive problems such as nausea and vomiting, constipation, diarrhoea or flatulence (wind).

Fibrates (eg ciprofibrate) work by affecting the way the liver acts on cholesterol. They are not as effective as other drugs at reducing cholesterol levels and can cause muscular pain, hair loss and stomach upsets; in some people they trigger the formation of gallstones through excess excretion of cholesterol into the bile.

Nicotinic acid derivatives (eg nicofuranose) work in two ways: by inhibiting the breakdown of stored body fat and by slowing down the production of fats in the liver. Side effects can include dilation of the blood vessels, causing dizziness, headaches and 'flushing' of the face; the side effects are severe enough to limit their usefulness.

Probucol is the only one of its type. Its action is not accurately known but it seems to encourage the liver to break down more cholesterol by increasing the excretion of bile acids in the stools. Side effects are mainly felt in the gut, causing flatulence (wind), abdominal pain or diarrhoea.

Surgical treatments

Insertion of a pacemaker

Each heartbeat is triggered by a tiny electrical signal (spark) that sends an electrical impulse along a conducting system (the equivalent of wires) to the pumping chambers of the heart. The sparking system should ensure that the heart beats regularly, but in some people the electrical system ceases to function correctly. (The fault may lie in the initial sparking centre or through a failure in transmission of the impulse; in either case the pumping chambers are not usually affected.) This is often due to coronary artery disease, although sometimes no cause may be found; a few people are born with an abnormality of conduction. The effect of the abnormality is failure to co-ordinate the contraction of the chambers. In severe cases the heart may be unable to pump blood effectively, and this can cause sudden death.

Symptoms that indicate there is a malfunction in the electrical system, causing heart rhythm disturbance (cardiac arrhythmia), can vary quite considerably. Some people may have defects that do not give any symptoms, whilst others experience dizziness and blackouts when the heart misses beats for short periods. A diagnosis is made from:

■ a description of the signs and symptoms; and
■ an ECG test (if a single test does not pick up a fault, a 24-hour monitor may be set up).

Fitting the pacemaker

In some cases a single treatment using an artificial electrical trigger (a defibrillator) may be all that is required to convert the heart rate to a more regular rhythm; more often, a device called a pacemaker is fitted to stimulate the heart to beat normally. A slim wire, called an electrode, is introduced into the heart via a vein in the shoulder or neck and then attached to a small box containing the pacemaker. The box holds long-lasting batteries and the electronic circuits that control the on and off switch to trigger the heartbeat. If the underlying condition is likely to improve with treatment (eg after a heart attack), a temporary pacemaker is fitted and carried outside the body. If the condition is unlikely to improve, a more permanent pacemaker is fitted – placed under the skin, usually below the collarbone.

After-care

Richard

'My wife and I felt nervous at first and she was very careful about giving me a hug, but we gradually relaxed. Making a few jokes about the extra weight and alien bodies helped to ease the tension.'

Immediately after a pacemaker has been inserted it is important to take care of the wound and avoid introducing any infection or undue stress to the area. Any signs of redness or swelling should be reported promptly. Your relative's doctor will advise about getting back to normal: most activities can be resumed after about a month, including exercise, driving and sexual contact. The pacemaker will be checked at the out-patients' clinic at regular intervals – more often in the early stages – until everyone is happy with the progress.

When you are caring for someone with a pacemaker, try to forget that it exists! In practice pacemakers rarely go wrong, the batteries last for up to 10 years and most modern electronic equipment, unless it is mal-functioning, should not cause any interference with the pacemaker. The wisest move you can make is to check that your relative carries a card giving all personal details about the pacemaker, and to be aware of the potential dangers of powerful electrical devices; for example, look out for warning signs usually displayed near security equipment at airports.

Heart valve replacement

The valves in the heart stop the blood from flowing backwards. Valvular problems may either be congenital (present at birth) or occur because the valves become diseased through illness or degeneration. In many older people the problem stems from an attack of rheumatic fever, a complication of a throat infection, suffered in childhood before the days of antibiotic treatment. The illness causes the valves to become weak and deformed. Any of the main valves can be affected, but it tends to be the mitral and aortic valves which are most prone to deterioration because they have to work the hardest. The mitral valve prevents the back-flow of blood between the upper and lower chambers on the left side of the heart, and the aortic valve does the same job where blood is pumped from the lower left chamber to go to the lungs. A diseased valve becomes constricted and weak, causing a number of problems:

- extra strain is placed on the heart to push the blood through a narrower channel;
- the muscle walls thicken to compensate;
- blood dams up, causing congestion;
- blood leaks backwards through the weakened valves; and
- fluid builds up in the lower half of the body, particularly in the abdomen and ankles, because of the problems caused by the harder work needed to pump the congested blood.

People with this condition are short of breath on exercise and sometimes on lying down in bed at night. They may also complain of tiredness and cough, occasionally producing blood. Clots may form in the malfunctioning heart and travel as emboli to the brain, where they cause a stroke.

Valve surgery

If the effects of a congenital condition are severe, surgical treatment will be necessary at an early stage in life. However, if rheumatic fever was the original cause of the deterioration, the need for treatment may not arise until much later in life. While the condition is not giving cause for concern, regular checks involving an ECG and a chest X-ray are sufficient to monitor the situation. If there is a deterioration, drug treatment may be started to relieve the congestion, reduce the work of the heart and regulate the heartbeat; this could be supplemented with a minor surgical procedure to stretch the mitral valve with a balloon device (angioplasty). Surgery is often recommended before the symptoms become severe and damage to the heart is irreparable.

The need for surgery is most common in the mitral valve. Abnormal valves can be either repaired or replaced. Replacement valves may be artificial mechanical devices or biological transplants from humans or pigs. Which type is chosen depends on the characteristics of the individual and the surgeon's opinion as to which will give the best outcome. There are a few minor differences in the two versions:

■ a mechanical valve clicks but a biological valve is silent;

■ a mechanical valve tends to create clots, so anticoagulant drugs must be taken permanently;

■ a biological valve requires anticoagulant drugs to be taken for a short period while it settles in; and

■ if a biological valve is used, a second operation could be necessary after 10–15 years (a mechanical valve lasts much longer). The risk of this must be weighed against the tedium of taking daily anticoagulant drugs and the need for regular checks at the outpatient anticoagulant clinic.

After-care

The long-term prospects after replacement surgery are generally excellent. Patients will be advised individually about diet, exercise and, if appropriate, returning to work. It is important to guard against undue risk of infection, because replacement heart valves are more susceptible to infection. In particular, infections can arise from bacteria that live in the mouth, so a high standard of dental care is necessary. Infection is especially likely after dental treatment or minor surgery. This dangerous complication can be prevented by taking antibiotics to 'cover' the procedure, so it is very important that the person tells the dentist or surgeon about the valve replacement.

Bypass surgery

Joan

'Peter had a heart attack four years after the angina started and he was admitted into hospital for a bypass operation within two weeks.'

This is now a common procedure carried out to replace coronary arteries that have become blocked by a build-up of fatty substances. The surgeon creates a bypass to allow fresh blood to flow through the coronary arteries, around the blockage. This is done by grafting in a blood vessel from another part of the patient's own body to create free-flowing routes in as many coronary arteries as necessary; from one to four is normal, depending on the level of disease.

After-care

> **Joan**
>
> 'The operation was fine and the hospital staff were good but follow-up was not so well organised. Looking back, I think we should have asked more questions but at the time we didn't know what to expect. Peter did get some continuing pain.'

Bypass operations are generally successful, especially in people without heart muscle damage from heart attacks. Untreated heart vessels and the graft itself may 'fur up' again, however, if the risk factors for atheroma are not dealt with.

Angioplasty

This technique is used to stretch the coronary artery in many patients with coronary heart disease. A long, fine tube is inserted into an artery in the groin and manoeuvred into position at the site of the blocked coronary artery. When correctly placed, the tip of the tube is inflated under high pressure (like a balloon) in order to create a wider passage in the artery to allow an increased blood flow.

Transplantation

In extreme and severe cases of chronic heart disease, a heart (and possibly lung) transplant would be considered for certain patients. Developments in surgical techniques and improvements in the drug therapy used to combat the rejection of a 'foreign' body part have made this option a practical possibility within recent years.

National Service Framework

The Department of Health published a National Service Framework for Coronary Heart Disease in 2000. The Framework is a 10-year programme which aims to improve standards of care and ensure that the same benefits are available to everyone across the country. It sets out 12 standards covering 7 different aspects of the disease and the steps that Primary Care Trusts should take to implement the NSF locally. For more information see *Good Service? The National Service Framework for Coronary Heart Disease*, which is a guide for people interested in how services for coronary heart disease in England are developed. It is published by the British Heart Foundation (see address on page 179) in association with the British Cardiac Patients Association.

Conclusion

This chapter has given basic information to help you and your relative understand how the heart and circulation work and has described some of the common conditions affecting many people today. The information has been technical in places, but knowing more about how the heart works will help you to understand why your relative has been ill. Tests are a necessary part of the diagnostic process and can be a frightening and unpleasant experience, particularly for someone who is feeling unwell, but many treatments cannot be started until the doctor has a clearer picture of the nature and extent of the problem.

As a carer you will probably accompany your relative to see the doctor, so it is vital that you also understand what is happening, to boost your confidence and improve the quality of care you provide. Most people in this situation feel anxious, so you are not alone if you find these visits daunting. Just remember that it's quite alright to ask questions about any aspect of the heart problem or care that you don't understand.

This chapter has also looked at some of the risk factors affecting other family members. If there seems to be a family history of heart disease, other family members should be aware of this and seek medical advice from an early age. Future chapters will help you and your relative make positive changes to daily living and help you think about your role and responsibilities as a carer.

For more information

ⓘ The British Heart Foundation publishes the **Heart Information Series** – a range of booklets on all problems and treatments relating to heart disease (address on page 179). Titles include:
Living with Heart Failure
Tests for Heart Conditions
Medicines for the Heart
Coronary Angioplasty and Coronary Bypass Surgery
Pacemakers.

ⓘ The 'Family Doctor' booklets *Understanding Cholesterol and Heart Disease* and *Understanding Blood Pressure* are available from many pharmacies/ chemist shops.

ⓘ **HEART UK** provides information on coronary heart disease and its management, including a 24-hour cholesterol and diet helpline and medical and nutritional advice (address on page 184).

ⓘ **The Stroke Association** (address on page 189) is a national charity which offers information and education services around the country.

2 Being a carer

A 'carer' is anyone who spends time and energy looking after another person who needs extra attention. This could be a friend or neighbour but is most likely to be a close family member, such as a spouse or parent. How you first became a carer will be unique to you. Most people start in one of three ways: following a dramatic event such as a heart attack; or because they have willingly prepared themselves for a change in role to take care of a partner or relative after, for example, a heart operation; others find they have entered into a caring situation over time, without being aware of major changes, as the health of a person close to them slowly deteriorates.

The word 'carer' in this context is intended to denote an 'informal' or 'non-professional' person, rather than a trained worker. Becoming a carer may lay you open to some strong, and perhaps confusing, feelings and it may take a while for you to adjust. This chapter offers information, advice and support to anyone who cares in some way for a spouse, relative or friend. It cannot give you all of the answers or solve all of your problems but it may help you to understand better some of the issues around caring in general.

What does it mean to be a carer?

Caring 'hours' can vary from a full-time activity if someone is seriously ill to as little as keeping a regular eye on their daily affairs. The aim of most carers is to help the person remain in their own home, leading a relatively independent life, for as long as possible. Wherever your position on the spectrum of care, it's likely that you are undertaking many of the jobs from the following list:

- providing a safe and comfortable home;
- doing practical jobs such as shopping, cooking, cleaning, laundry and gardening;
- giving personal care and basic nursing procedures;
- offering love, emotional support and company;
- providing help and advice on running personal affairs; and
- reducing isolation and bringing a bit of the 'outside world' into the daily life of someone who can no longer get out and about.

Fact Box

- Over 6 million people in the UK look after a relative or friend who cannot manage without help because of illness, frailty or disability.
- 10 per cent of the total population, or about 12 per cent of the adult population, have a caring role.
- More women (3.9 million: 18 per cent) than men (2.9 million: 14 per cent) are carers.
- The peak age for becoming a carer is between 45 and 64 years (25 per cent of adults in this age group).
- 1.7 million carers provide care for 20 hours or more every week. 27 per cent of these are aged 65 years or over.
- 70 per cent of those cared for are 65 years or over.
- 14 per cent of carers say that they have 'given up work to care'.

(continued)

- 51 per cent of carers provide personal care to someone within their own home; 22 per cent administer medicines; 71 per cent give other practical help.
- The financial costs of caring are significant; 77 per cent of carers who responded to a survey by Carers UK said that they were financially 'worse off'.
- Six out of ten carers felt that caring was affecting their own health. A further study found that over 20 per cent of carers providing over 20 hours of care a week had a mental health problem themselves.

(Source: *Facts About Carers*, Carers UK, May 2003.)

Recognising yourself as a carer

Joan

'Peter had angina, a heart attack and a heart bypass operation, so I suppose I was a carer. I never thought of it like that.'

You may not think of yourself as a carer because you undertake your tasks out of love and friendship, and you may have fallen into the caring role because no one else is available. Many carers do not recognise themselves as such and therefore do not seek information or know how to look for further help. It is vital that you be aware that support and help are available, and that you have choices and rights as a carer that go alongside the responsibilities.

There are more than 6 million carers in the UK, nearly 2 million of whom provide substantial amounts of care. At times being a carer creates tremendous anxiety and distress: you may be undertaking tasks that feel difficult and unfamiliar; you are largely unpaid and untrained; and you are often on duty for 24 hours a day, seven days a week. Much will be expected of you, and this responsibility will tax your patience. In taking on an enduring commitment, you need to pace yourself, use a range of skills and experience, build up strong physical and mental systems, and maintain a good sense of humour. You won't always get it right – life is never completely straightforward and free from pressure – but there are many sources of support you can draw on to help things run smoothly. Chapters 6 and 7 tell you more about managing stress and finding ways to cope with very difficult situations.

Your perceptions and feelings as a carer

Penny, a carers' support worker

'Try to understand that feeling guilty, anxious and angry are usual emotions and reactions. They are often signs that carers need to consider a period of respite. It's easy to say "don't worry", but try not to waste time doing so.'

You will have your ups and downs and there will be days when you feel you cannot cope. Even if you actively chose your caring situation, this will not stop you from having negative feelings, and although most people decide to care willingly, this will not be true of every carer. Professional people who work with carers understand that carers feel a range of very conflicting emotions and that sometimes they express these feelings towards their relative and towards the people who offer them support.

Anger, frustration, fear, resentment and guilt often exist alongside other emotions such as sadness, love, anxiety and concern. Powerful emotions can drain and exhaust you, so try not to add 'worry' to the list. Worry and guilt are two emotions that cause much wasted energy. Look instead at problems from a positive angle – if you feel in control, you will cope well; if the problem is not within your control, spending time being worried or guilty won't improve the situation and may even prevent your finding a solution. It's often hard for carers to understand that they may have been bottling up a range of strong emotions but that it's absolutely OK to feel this way. Relieving the unhappy feelings is better than storing them up.

It is still assumed in society today that a blood-tie or marriage relationship automatically makes a person (usually the woman in the partnership) the main carer and that in this role she must undertake a number of onerous, unpaid tasks. You may believe this yourself. It is often assumed by others that you have the ability to cope and that your capacity to care can stretch to meet all the demands that are placed on you. You may feel that other people expect so much from you – family members, GPs, social workers – and that you cannot let them down.

To help you come to terms with your role as a carer, it's important that you think about all of these expectations, including what you expect of yourself. If you feel confused or overwhelmed by the enormity of the task, talking to someone – perhaps another carer – might help. Look at the list below and tick off the feelings that have crossed your mind in recent weeks:

- lack of confidence and low feeling of self-worth;
- no credentials to do the job you are doing;
- worried about shortage of money;
- lack of recognition/status;
- not sure where to turn for allies or support;
- bewildered by the maze of services;
- unclear about what you can ask for;
- feel your own needs are always disregarded in favour of your relative; and
- no time or space to be yourself.

These thoughts are very common, even if they have been only fleeting. Don't block them out. Accept that occasionally carers do feel unable to carry on and sometimes they are forced to take dramatic steps to make their voice heard. Support workers should do everything in their power to ease your position and avert a crisis. Unfortunately, not all carers have access to an adequate support system. If this applies to you, do speak to your GP or the duty social worker from the local authority's social services department and ask about additional help before crisis point is reached.

Setting boundaries

Janet, a carers' support worker

'People often become carers in a situation without being aware that carers do have choices.'

How did you become a carer? Did it creep up on you slowly over the years or happen suddenly because of a crisis? Whatever the original reason, at some point it is vital that you sit back and take stock of the current situation. Ask yourself a few searching questions and think logically and seriously about the answers. Talk to a counsellor (see Chapter 6) if an unbiased listener will help you sort out your feelings.

Ask yourself:

- Why am I doing this job?
- Am I being pressured by other people?
- Will I feel that I have rejected someone I love if I stop?
- Is the caring situation going to be long or short term?
- Do I want to continue or to pass the responsibility over to others?
- What are my options for change?

As a carer you must make a conscious decision about whether to continue with caring, because making a definite choice will help you to cope with the task, however difficult. There may be times when carers feel in despair, but when they perceive that they have no choice, that they were pressured into the situation by others or that they did not fully consider the seriousness of the situation, they are more likely to become angry, resentful and suffer ill-health. There is nothing wrong with saying 'no' if you already feel over-burdened. If you cannot continue

35

to care for your relative at home, you can still continue to be involved with their care elsewhere.

How 'good' is your caring situation?

Researchers studying informal caring, given by close relatives, have identified a model of a good caring situation that is recognised by professional people as an important factor in maintaining a positive and healthy lifestyle for the key people involved. Whilst acknowledging that no caring situation can hope to fulfil the ideal all of the time, it is important that everyone accepts the value of such a model and works towards achieving this as a goal.

The model list

- The carer makes a conscious choice whether or not to care.
- The carer is able to recognise their own limits and needs.
- The carer lives close by, but not in the same house.
- A network of care is set up, so that responsibility is shared.
- The carer has time to themselves and doesn't have to give up too much of their own life.
- The carer has access to information and help to learn skills.
- A good past relationship existed between the carer and the person being cared for.
- The dependent person wishes to stay as independent as possible.
- The dependent person retains their own friends.
- The carer fosters independence in the dependent person.
- Everybody keeps a sense of humour.
- Professional help is there when it is needed.
- The carer feels supported and valued.

What formal support is available for carers?

Increasingly the rights and needs of carers are being taken into account, although it has taken many years of lobbying by pressure groups and individual people and changes in legislation to reach the stage we are at now. The most relevant pieces of legislation are summarised below, and the National Service Framework for older people is explained on page 80. Local authority documents such as a community care charter may include information on help for carers and carers' rights. If you need a more detailed explanation of the rights and services to which you are entitled, contact your local social services department (social work department in Scotland), which will be listed in the telephone directory.

State provision

NHS and Community Care Act 1990

The NHS and Community Care Act brought together many pieces of legislation that date back to 1948 and is designed to help meet the care needs of older people and those with learning and physical disabilities and mental health problems, preferably in their own home or the area where they live. Social services take the lead role and work together with the NHS and voluntary organisations to offer a broad range of services for people in need and their carers. The services cannot promise to meet all needs, because community care is subject to certain eligibility criteria (see pages 82–83 and 85) but a trained person will assess the needs of the person you care for and then, if that person is eligible, arrange appropriate services in what is known as a 'care package'. The services (care package) arranged through social services are means-tested.

Carers (Recognition and Services) Act 1995

This Act came into force on 1 April 1996. It defines a carer as 'someone who provides (or intends to provide) a substantial amount of care on a regular basis'. It contains two main elements that deal with the rights of carers: to ask for a separate assessment of their needs when the person they care for is being assessed or reassessed; and the duty of the local authority to take into consideration the findings of this assessment when deciding which services to offer the person being cared for. (There is more information about assessments in Chapter 4 on pages 81–83.)

37

The Act requires social services departments, if requested to do so by a carer, to assess the ability of the carer to provide, or to continue to provide, care, and to take this into account when deciding what services to provide to the person being cared for. To qualify for an assessment a carer must be providing (or intending to provide) regular and substantial care, and the person they care for must be being assessed by social services at the same time. Because there is no official definition of 'regular' and 'substantial', each caring situation will be assessed individually. The assessment should recognise the carer's knowledge of the person, and the responsibility for the caring situation should be agreed as a shared undertaking between the carer and the social services department.

Carers UK

'The Carers (Recognition and Services) Act 1995 has been one of the most significant developments in the history of the carers' movement. Not only did it recognise the rights of carers for the first time, but the campaign which led to the Carers Act showed the level of agreement there was about the rights and needs of carers.'

Carers and Disabled Children Act 2000

This Act extends the right to assessment, giving carers the right to have their own needs assessed even if the cared-for person does not want to be assessed. Following such an assessment services can be provided to the carer, whereas under the previous 1995 Act services which take account of the needs of the carer are provided to the cared for person. Carers can now also receive direct payments (ie cash payments in lieu of services which social services assess you as needing) under the same legislation.

Carers (Equal Opportunities) Act 2004

This Act builds on the above legislation by requiring local authorities to inform carers of their right to assessment where the cared for person is being assessed or where the local authority is otherwise aware that the carer might be entitled to an assessment. The assessment must consider whether the carer is, or wishes to, work or undertake training, education or any leisure activity. If, as a result of assessment, the local authority concludes that another agency, such as the NHS, might be able to assist the carer in meeting their needs they must inform the agency who must then give due consideration to the request.

Charters

Social services departments publish charters which aim to tell people what they can expect from the agencies that provide 'community care' services for adults. These charters, across the country, have been given the collective title *Better Care, Higher Standards*. The various charters have been drawn up to reflect the standards and targets that have been set by health care trusts, social services and housing departments in order to fulfil local need, so the content will differ slightly from area to area. Basically, however, the charters fall into two types, which are summarised below. Contact your social services office to enquire about local versions.

Charters for carers

These charters usually acknowledge the valuable role carers perform in caring for someone at home. They state that practical help is a key priority for social services departments and set out how the department aims to respond to typical requests expressed by carers. The charters offer:

- opportunities for sharing experiences;
- recognition for carers;
- practical help;
- information and advice;
- advice about welfare benefits; and
- a short break from caring.

Community care charters

These charters complement the community care plan and are concerned with the services that help people to remain in their own homes. They cover:

- being able to get in touch with the appropriate person;
- understanding people's needs;
- planning care;
- dealing with unmet needs;
- the services people can expect to receive;
- how to access information;
- what to do if things go wrong; and
- relationships with people receiving services.

Both types of charter will be concerned with telling people about the services they can expect to receive for home care, personal help and care in care homes and how they can gain access to services more easily.

Older people are represented on the independent, statutory patients' forums, which are being set up in every health trust area, so that patients can have their say about how local NHS services are run.

Being informed

Penny, a carers' support worker

'Information is often thrown at carers when they are desperate, rather than when they can listen calmly. It's much better to "drip feed" small amounts when it is needed than for the carer to have to try to remember everything at once.'

Janet, a carers' support worker

'Take a pen and paper with you when you visit the surgery or a professional person and make notes. GPs and social workers seem very busy to people who are frightened and anxious, but take your time.'

If you are new to caring, it may help to speak to a social worker to find out what services are available in your area and generally make yourself known, even if at this stage your needs are not great and you would not qualify for specific help. If you have been looking after your relative for a while, the time may come when your caring situation changes, and being informed is a major factor in maintaining control and dealing with difficult issues. Knowing something about what might be offered will make a basic starting point when you seek additional support. Don't try to remember everything you are told but do try to make a note of the key headings that services fall under; for example, your rights as a carer, domestic help, where you can obtain equipment. Set up an information folder and keep a notebook if it will help to organise your affairs. Information about the provision of services for older people and carers is given more fully in Chapter 4, which advises carers about how to cope with failing health.

Carers UK

'When carers have an assessment, they get more services.'

Your own health needs

Don't forget to look after your own health and well-being. This may sound like a tall order but you do need to maintain your own strength:

- Eat regularly and properly – if you are preparing meals for someone else, try not to skimp on your own food.
- Take regular breaks from caring, even if you only find time to walk in the garden or read a book. Plan longer breaks at regular intervals.
- Arrange time away from the house to meet other people, because isolation can be a major problem for many carers. There are sitting services available that will send a volunteer to stay with your relative – ask your local Age Concern.
- Learn to move your relative safely, because strained and injured backs are a great problem for carers who are suddenly thrust into a caring role. Ask your community nurse or social worker about training courses or equipment.

- Take cat naps during the day if sleep at night is disturbed – without feeling guilty.
- Ask about help with housework or gardening if you are over-tired. Some local authorities and voluntary organisations run gardening schemes.

Carers' support centres and workers

Penny, a carers' support worker

'Before you meet a professional person, jot down a few notes as it's important to ask the questions that are right for you. Try not to make assumptions about what you think may be available – people are often surprised at the amount of services that exist.'

There are many schemes set up around the country specifically to provide help and support for carers. They are run mainly by health and social services teams and voluntary organisations. The workers understand the problems and feelings of isolation experienced by carers and are specially trained to help carers receive relevant and up-to-date information, gain access to services and welfare benefits and guide them in their caring role. Support workers welcome contact with you as a carer and will listen to your hopes, concerns and fears. Many produce newsletters, run local support groups for carers and have drop-in and respite care facilities.

Freda, a social worker

'We understand that carers get to the end of their tether and may be quite close to physical and mental collapse at times; occasionally it is their relative who takes the brunt of their anxieties and anger. Tension is usually relieved through shouting, but carers can lose their temper more violently. If you feel it's time to look at ways of relieving the strain, then do seek help before you reach crisis point. If you feel really desperate, give the Samaritans a call.'

Emergency help

Carers often express fears about what to do if there is an accident and their relative falls. The advice from the ambulance service is: dial 999 for help. Do not attempt to move the person, as they will need to be assessed for injury.

First aid

If a situation occurs that needs prompt first aid, try to think and act calmly. You will be more effective and better able to reassure your relative.

If your relative falls, collapses or becomes seriously ill, either call an ambulance yourself or ask someone to do this for you. Then treat your relative according to their state of consciousness, until help arrives.

If conscious:

■ Reassure your relative that help is on the way.
■ If your relative has difficulty breathing or complains of chest pains, gently raise them to a half-sitting position, with the head and shoulders supported.
■ If your relative feels faint, sit them down, leaning forwards with their head between their knees. Encourage them to take deep breaths, but not to over-breathe because this can quickly cause dizziness for other reasons.
■ If your relative has fallen, do not move them unnecessarily as this may cause further injury.
■ If your relative has diabetes, give them a sugary drink or a sugar lump or other sweet food.
■ Do *not* give anything to eat or drink if your relative does not have diabetes.

If unconscious:

■ If possible, lie your relative on the floor on their side; otherwise try to position the head with the jaw forwards in order to maintain a clear airway and to prevent saliva and the tongue falling backwards.

- Do *not* try to remove dentures, because poking about in the mouth of an unconscious person is likely to do more harm than good.
- Loosen tight clothing.
- Cover your relative with a blanket to keep them warm.
- Do *not* give any food or fluids of any kind.

If you become ill or need extra help

If you become ill and need additional help during the day, you can contact the duty social services officer or your GP. For assistance outside office hours, contact the social services emergency duty team or a medical answering service. (Look up the numbers in the telephone directory and put them by the telephone now.)

Carer's emergency card

You might be concerned that you could have an accident or be taken ill while you are away from home, leaving the person you care for alone. You can obtain an emergency identity card that gives information about you as a carer so that your relative will not be left unattended. Cards are available from Carers UK (address on page 180).

Conclusion

This chapter has offered material to help you focus on your role as a carer and given you an insight into the nature of caring. Reading the information may have been painful for you, especially if it raised uncomfortable questions that you found difficult to answer. Hopefully, if you are one of the many carers who are unfamiliar with the official system, it will encourage you to seek support and ask for an assessment of your caring situation. The statistics in the Fact Box at the beginning of the chapter give you a clear indication that you are not alone in the caring business. Take comfort in the fact that the predicament of carers is now under open discussion and their efforts are being increasingly recognised and supported.

For more information

i CarersLine is a telephone helpline, run by Carers UK, which offers a wide range of information to carers. It operates nationally for the cost of a local call. Lines are open Monday to Friday, 10am–noon and 2pm–4pm on 0808 808 7777.

i Age Concern Factsheets (see page 197 for details of how to obtain factsheets):
6 *Finding Help at Home*
24 *Direct Payments from Social Services*
41 *Local Authority Assessment for Community Care Services*
46 *Paying for Care and Support at Home.*

i **Counsel and Care** Factsheet 10 *Help for Carers* (address on page 181).

i *Coping with Caring*, a free leaflet available from many pharmacies/chemist shops.

3 Daily living

The risk factors for coronary heart disease were outlined in Chapter 1. Although gender and family history are fixed, many others can be lessened by making changes in lifestyle, and this chapter discusses how this may be done. Many of the recommendations are aimed at lowering high blood pressure, to reduce strain on the heart – especially if blood vessels are already clogged with fatty deposits.

Changes include:

- improving the diet, to lower blood cholesterol levels and reduce obesity;

- taking more exercise, to keep the heart muscle fit;

- giving up smoking, to reduce by half the chances of having a heart attack; and

- managing stress (Chapters 6 and 7 offer help with reducing anxiety levels).

Many people are concerned about the effect of a heart condition on sexual relationships and are unsure how to ask professional people for advice. This chapter gives some answers, and if you or your relative are still uncertain you can use the information to help ask a few personal questions. Not all of the changes will apply to the person you care for but the information could be useful for other family members, especially if an increased risk of heart problems runs in the family. The thought of making major lifestyle changes on top of everything else that has happened may be daunting, so the chapter starts by offering some tips about making changes in general.

Making changes

Sylvia

'I was relieved when the doctor told us that there were lots of things we could do to help prevent another heart attack. It's easier to cope if you think you are helping.'

Celia, an occupational therapist

'The value of rehabilitation must not be underestimated, as the majority of heart attacks are survived.'

Any heart condition is serious; if you were with your relative at the time of a heart attack, you are probably afraid that it might happen again. Most people feel anxious during the convalescent stage and need reassurance that ordinary life can resume. Lots of support will be available in the early days to help you both begin the process of getting back to normal. Looking after someone who is ill brings responsibilities, and you will want to do your best for your relative in every possible way. Follow the advice given by professional people and you and your relative will soon slip into a new pattern of life.

Fact Box

Here are a few positive facts to help your relative overcome any anxieties:

- Most people make an excellent recovery after a heart attack.
- Most people are fitter after they have introduced changes to their lifestyle – improved diet, increased exercise and relaxation.
- The heart, like any other part of the body, is designed to repair itself and can compensate for some damage that is not life-threatening.
- After heart surgery or a heart attack, it is normal to tire more easily and this is not necessarily a sign that things are going wrong.
- Self-help is a great boost to recovery.

Elsie and Tom

'After the heart attack, the occupational therapist told us to stop, take stock and think carefully about how we were running our lives and what our hectic lifestyle was doing to our bodies.'

A change in circumstances is always triggered by some event, however minor. If you think about major changes in the past, something happened that set you off on a new course of action. Sometimes the event is not within your control and you feel unsettled until you have come to terms with the new situation. The process is easier to deal with if you allow time to work your way naturally through a series of stages.

The first period is often called the *unfreezing* stage. It's the time to let everything settle down and accept that you can't put the clock back. It's important that you both spend time talking about how your relative's illness has changed your lives: don't try to block out any feelings, because you won't be able to plan for the future while you still feel upset about what has happened. Allow yourself to grieve about the past; it's perfectly normal to want to do this when a traumatic event has taken place. Let relatives and friends offer support.

The next stage is about *moving forward*. It's the time to start making changes. Your relative will be on the road to recovery and you will both feel ready to plan for the future. Don't rush this stage, and talk to other people if you feel anxious about making decisions. Your plans might cover a range of issues – financial, health and practical matters. They all need careful thought.

When you and your relative have made decisions and begun to sort out the practical issues, you are entering stage three; this time is called the *re-freezing* period. It becomes *solid* when you both feel comfortable about the changes that have taken place. This final stage won't happen swiftly, so don't be alarmed or feel there is something wrong if it takes a while before life feels close to normal again. Be honest with yourselves about accepting the changes, because pretending and putting on a brave face when you feel anxious inside can be stressful. Better times will return eventually.

Sylvia

'I will always remember the occupational therapist saying to me "Understanding makes coping easier".'

If you or your relative are having difficulty accepting that change is taking place, it might help to talk about what is holding you up. Sometimes problems are perceived to be greater than they really are. It often happens that, as soon as you think you have dealt with a 'worry', it springs up again in another guise. This may be because you haven't truly come to terms with the problem, so it continues to dominate your thoughts. The change process is a slow business, so don't rush into a false sense of acceptance. As you resolve problems, bit by bit, the nightmare of dealing with a huge change will feel less of a burden. Follow these guidelines for the future:

- Do look forward.
- Do make a list of the good things in life – however trivial.
- Do talk to someone about difficult decisions.

49

- Do accept that life moves forward.
- Do acknowledge your own feelings and find someone to talk to if you feel the need.
- Do remember that help is available.
- Don't rush yourselves.
- Don't bottle up feelings.
- Don't feel guilty.
- Don't try to place blame.
- Don't look over your shoulder, hankering for a 'better' past.

Diet

Sylvia

'I've learned to look after myself, too. It's important that I keep going, so I try to get enough sleep and to eat properly.'

Rita, a dietitian

'"Variety is the spice of life". This is particularly true in terms of diet – taking a wide variety of food can ensure health needs are met.'

Diet is an important factor in any programme designed to reduce the risk of coronary heart disease. A review of what your relative eats will be high on the list of changes that you will need to help them make. Dietary advice is readily available for patients after heart surgery or a heart attack. Talk to the practice nurse, who will have a selection of leaflets, and ask the GP if your relative can be referred to a dietitian for specific advice tailored to their needs. The information below outlines the links between food and heart disease.

Obesity (very overweight)

Excess weight causes a great strain on the whole body, especially the heart and joints. Overweight people are more likely to have raised blood pressure and an increased risk of developing diabetes as well as heart and circulatory (cardiovascular) diseases. Many heart problems – angina attacks, high levels of cholesterol and high blood pressure – improve considerably when extra weight is shed. Some people even reduce their need for medication.

Rita, a dietitian

'Watch your weight! Don't let it creep up – it's much harder to take off than put on.'

Over the years, slimming has become a fashionable, money-making business with a number of unsuitable 'crash' diets being promoted by their manufacturers and ill-informed press articles. Unfortunately, miracle diets don't work for more than a short time and many are unsafe. They rely heavily on starving the body of food rather than encouraging dieters to change their poor eating habits through a balanced and sensible eating plan. The only effective way to lose weight permanently is to eat the amount required by the body to balance its daily energy needs – too much and our bodies store the excess calories as fat for use in future emergencies.

Some people inherit a tendency to be a certain shape and gain weight more readily than others. Nevertheless, anyone who eats fewer calories than they burn up will lose weight, especially if they link their healthy diet to getting sufficient exercise. When trying to cut back on calories, it's important not to lose valuable vitamins and minerals in the process. In everyday terms this means selecting foods that give a high nutritional value per calorie. When shopping or eating out choose:

■ more fruit and vegetables to increase the fibre, vitamins and minerals;
■ moderate amounts of starchy (carbohydrate) foods (bread, rice, pasta), because they fill you up and contain no more calories than

51

protein (remember that unwanted carbohydrates are stored up but excess proteins are not);

■ wholemeal versions rather than white or processed foods, because they contain more fibre, vitamins and minerals;

■ less fatty foods, because fat is twice as high in calories as the same weight of starch or protein;

■ less sugary foods such as sweet drinks, cakes and biscuits, because these foods contain high-energy calories but no true food value; you can cut down on sugar without losing any nourishment;

■ less salt, because too much salt can lead to high blood pressure, thus increasing the risk of strokes and heart disease; and

■ less alcohol, because this has a higher calorie content than starch or protein.

A lot of benefit can be gained by making minor changes. It's important to continue to enjoy food, so don't make dramatic changes overnight. Introduce new foods and cooking methods gradually and buy a variety of foods so that a nutritious balance is maintained.

Rita, a dietitian

'Keep your interest in food – it's never too late to try new foods, new tastes and new styles of cooking.'

Blood cholesterol levels

The risk of coronary heart disease is directly linked to levels of cholesterol in the blood. The higher the level of total cholesterol, the higher the risk. Too much cholesterol in the blood causes a build-up of deposits on artery walls. The cholesterol circulating in the bloodstream comes from two sources: it is produced by your body and it is absorbed from foods that naturally contain the substance. Some people inherit a tendency towards high levels of blood cholesterol. If this is a family problem, it would be wise for younger family members to seek advice from a doctor and have a blood cholesterol test.

Cholesterol is an oily substance that plays an important part in the make-up and work of body cells. Most cholesterol found in the blood is produced by the liver, and is carried to tissues in the body by substances (called lipoproteins) in the bloodstream. The main sources of foods naturally rich in cholesterol are eggs, liver, kidneys and some shellfish. However, don't rush to cut out these foods, unless recommended by a doctor or dietitian.

The most important point to understand when reviewing diet is the overall *amount and type* of fat eaten rather than the actual cholesterol itself. Some fats are essential for good health and others are harmful. Foods high in **saturated** fats increase blood cholesterol levels, whereas foods high in **polyunsaturated** and **monounsaturated** fats can help to reduce it. Don't worry about trying to understand the scientific words for different types of fat; if you follow the guidelines below it will be easy to cut back on harmful fats and to eat those that help reduce cholesterol levels.

Saturated fats are found mainly in the following foods, and tend to be solid in consistency:

- meat (including meat products) – beef, lamb, pork, suet, lard and dripping;
- dairy products: milk, butter, cream and cheese; and
- some vegetable oils and hard margarines containing coconut and palm oils that have been specially treated to make them solid.

Unsaturated fats are found in the following foods and oils, and tend to be soft or liquid in consistency:

- vegetable oils: sunflower, corn, soya, rapeseed and olive;
- soft margarines: all labelled 'high in polyunsaturated fat'; and
- certain foods: nuts and oily fish such as tuna, mackerel, sardines, salmon and trout.

If you are unsure about the type of fat a product contains, check the label – all foods carry a description of the contents. Manufacturers are keen to promote healthy foods, so the word 'polyunsaturated' will be prominent on the packaging. Reducing the overall amount of fat that is consumed is the main goal, because this will help lower weight as well as cholesterol levels.

Tips to reduce fat

■ Use skimmed or semi-skimmed milk rather than full-cream milk.

■ Trim off all the visible fat from meat and choose as lean a cut as you can afford.

■ Minced meats always have a higher fat content than large cuts.

■ Cut down on the amount of meat products you buy, especially sausages, salami and meat pies, because their fat content is often very high.

■ Change to low-fat versions of dairy products; cottage and Dutch cheeses are good, and look for the word 'polyunsaturates' when you choose soft margarines and spreads.

■ Eat more fish and poultry of any variety.

■ Remove the skin from poultry.

■ Drain away all excess fat during the cooking process.

■ If you frequently use a deep fat fryer or pan, gradually change over to other methods that exclude fat rather than using extra: grilling meats and poaching or microwaving fish in a little milk with lots of pepper are easy ways to start.

■ Cut out completely fatty snacks such as crisps and biscuits: bring in fruit and yoghurt for puddings or eating between meals.

Rita, a dietitian

'Eat regularly. Start the day well with breakfast, but remember "healthy eating" guidelines and lose the frying pan.'

Salt (sodium chloride)

There has been pressure from dietitians in the past to cut down on the amount of salt in the diet because too much contributes to high blood pressure, increasing the risk of heart and kidney disease and strokes.

Most people eat far more salt than their body requires, some up to ten times as much as they need. About half comes from processed foods (tinned foods, pies, cooked meats), about one quarter is added at the cooking stage and at the table, and the remainder is naturally present in foods. Salt intake can be reduced in lots of ways and very soon taste buds will adjust to the change; aim to reduce total consumption to a maximum of one teaspoonful per day, not forgetting the hidden salt in tinned foods.

It is difficult to calculate the amount of salt in canned food because it may be present in different forms; for example, brine, monosodium glutamate and soy sauce are used to enhance flavour. The best advice is to use processed food sparingly because you have less control over the salt content than foods prepared at home. A study at Duke University in the USA found that the added salt content of processed foods can be reduced significantly by rinsing them under running water. Green beans rinsed for one minute lost 41 per cent of their sodium content, and tuna fish lost even more. The salt content of most condiments and seasonings is also high. For example, one teaspoon of table salt contains about 1,965 mg of sodium chloride compared with 1,716 mg in one tablespoon of soy sauce.

Tips to reduce salt

- Gradually reduce the amount added to food during cooking and increase other flavours such as herbs, spices and lemon juice to change and highlight flavours.
- Reduce the number of snack foods that are obviously coated in salt (eg crisps and salted nuts); this will also cut down on fat intake, so is a double bonus.
- Try hard not to add salt at the table. Taste first and add salt sparingly if necessary but preferably try something else; lemon juice and black pepper both enhance taste.
- Cut salted, processed foods (eg meat pies, bacon, gammon, tinned foods in brine) completely out of the diet if possible – there are lots of fresh alternatives.

■ Look at the packaging and buy foods that are labelled 'no added salt'; many food producers are aware of the health risks and 'healthy' products are readily available.

Rita, a dietitian

'Fluids are important; don't restrict them unless your doctor says so. Aim for eight cups per day, including water, fruit juice and hot drinks.'

Alcohol

Small amounts of alcohol (one or two drinks per day) may be beneficial in reducing the risks of heart disease. Heavy drinking, however, raises blood pressure and increases risks. Alcohol 'bingeing' – drinking large amounts in one bout – is also not good for the system, because the liver must work very hard to clear the toxic substances from the body. The best policy is to keep within the recommended limits of 14 units per week for women and 20 units per week for men. A 'unit' or standard drink is equivalent to a pub measure:

beer	½ pint
wine	1 standard glass
spirits	1 standard measure

One group of scientists has suggested that small quantities of alcohol could be good for people with heart problems because it helps the arteries to dilate, enabling the blood to flow more freely. This thinking has led many health writers and doctors to promote moderate alcohol consumption as desirable, especially red wine. However, it is important to look also at the other side of the story, which shows a different picture. Another group of scientists researching the causes of high blood pressure found a close link between alcohol and hypertension. The results of their studies seem to show that the more alcohol people drank, the greater their risk of high blood pressure. This information contradicted previous thinking, and therefore needed some explanation, because the obvious conclusion should have been that if alcohol dilates blood vessels then blood pressure ought to fall, not increase. Further evidence has indicated that the raised blood pressure was caused by the direct effect of alcohol on the heart muscle. The people who took part in this study, and who drank in moderation, were shown to have enlarged hearts and high blood pressure.

In the face of all the evidence from many studies throughout the world, the strongest message for everyone is that alcohol should be drunk in moderation. It is still strongly linked to many other causes of illness and death – liver disease, stroke, cancer and accidental death – and there is no firm evidence that it prevents heart disease. Everyone (even people who do not have a heart problem) is advised to restrict their drinking by having at least two or three alcohol-free days each week to give their bodies a rest.

For people with existing heart problems the advice is more definite: ask your doctor for guidelines about drinking, because circumstances vary with the individual. Alcohol may make the situation worse rather than better for anyone who suffers from heart problems. However, with the doctor's permission, alcohol need not be banned completely; the indications are that drinking *small, well-controlled* amounts will do no lasting harm. Have an occasional glass of wine but stay well below the recommended levels for people without heart problems, and avoid situations where a large, rich meal is accompanied by several drinks and over-excitement. This combination of events is more likely to put pressure on an over-stressed heart. You can encourage your relative to enjoy the party but stay in control. For people who experience difficulties in cutting back on alcohol, local and national organisations offer self-help groups and counselling to help gain control of the problem: look in the telephone directory, ask at the Citizens Advice Bureau or contact Drinkline (address on page 183).

Tips to reduce alcohol

For your relative:

- Set a reasonable limit (get medical advice about drinking levels), and don't be persuaded to binge.
- Be firm about saying 'no' when drinking with friends – explain why but don't feel that an apology is necessary.
- To cut down on drinking, sip drinks slowly, miss out rounds and choose alcohol-free drinks to quench thirst.

For you:

- If your relative was a regular heavy drinker either at the pub or at home, encourage them to change their habits; if they are bored or stressed alcohol shouldn't be used to blur the issues.
- If your relative needs to drink less alcohol but is finding it difficult to cut back, remind them of the long-term benefits/risks; ask family and friends for support and talk to a counsellor yourself if the going is really tough.

For both of you:

- When pouring out drinks at home, be very aware of the size of the glass – home measures tend to be more generous than pub measures and many people underestimate the strength of some beers and lagers.
- Think about ways of having a treat with the money that is being saved: little rewards are good for the morale.

Smoking

Celia, an occupational therapist

'Smoking – quit for life, *your* life.'

Tobacco is the substance most linked to the cause of coronary heart disease. It is a myth that smoking may not be harmful. The evidence from a large number of scientific studies shows that all forms of smoking damage health: cigarettes, cigars and pipes. (Lifelong pipe smokers don't inhale, so the tar is deposited around the mouth, which is where they get cancer; people who previously smoked cigarettes and change to a pipe tend to continue to inhale, so their risk of lung cancer remains, to which they add risk in the mouth.) A person who smokes cigarettes greatly increases their risk of high blood pressure and is twice as likely as a non-smoker to have a heart attack. It's never too late to feel the benefits of giving up, however, and it's the most effective change that anyone who suffers from a heart problem can make to improve their health.

Tobacco smoke contains many poisonous chemicals that play a significant part in the build-up of atherosclerosis, the process that 'hardens' and 'furs up' the artery walls. Moreover, chemical action makes the blood thicker, increasing the chance of blood clots. The most serious damage is caused by three main substances:

- **Carbon monoxide** This takes the place of some of the oxygen in the bloodstream, so vital organs are deprived of essential oxygen. Carbon monoxide also aggravates arterial disease, contributing to high blood pressure.
- **Tar** This lines the tissues of the lungs, reducing the amount of oxygen getting across to the bloodstream. Tar also causes irritation and inflammation of the lungs, leading to the development of chronic bronchitis and emphysema, two conditions that can eventually contribute to heart failure. (And, of course, there is the risk of developing lung cancer.)
- **Nicotine** This is an addictive substance that acts as a mental depressant but its chief danger is its ability to act swiftly on artery walls, causing them to contract very strongly. These muscle spasms vastly reduce the flow of blood to the heart muscle and are the major cause of angina.

Most people understand and accept that smoking is bad for their health, especially people with heart disease. If the person you are caring for has been in hospital, they will have been told of the dangers and may already have given up. This is not an easy thing to do, because long-term smokers are usually addicted to the nicotine and will suffer withdrawal symptoms. Stopping smoking can be difficult during convalescence when factors such as boredom, fear of recurrent illness, and anxiety about the future, increase levels of stress. Be ready to offer encouragement, as you can help in lots of ways.

Tips to stop smoking

■ Listen to your relative and try not to criticise any lapses: be sympathetic but firm.

■ Don't suggest that your relative start smoking again – however irritable they become!

■ Talk to other former smokers or telephone the freephone helpline run by the independent charity Quitline (0800 002 200) that provides confidential and practical advice for people wanting to give up smoking.

■ Change routines so that old habits don't make it easy to light up – suggest that your relative sits in a different chair, drinks tea instead of coffee and does something different after a meal – all times when a cigarette might have been smoked. Identify danger times/places and alter behaviour if necessary.

■ Offer plenty of water, fruit and fruit juice, because ex-smokers need to flush the chemicals well out of their system – the vitamin C helps rid the body of nicotine. Be careful, though, not to increase calorie intake with foods that have a high sugar content.

■ Help reduce nicotine cravings by weaning off tobacco products using nicotine patches and chewing gum.

■ Suggest different forms of entertainment to help cope with the boredom, particularly things that use the hands.

■ Chat about the money that is being saved and think of ways to treat yourselves.

- Offer plenty of praise and support but don't overdo the sympathy; some sensitive people would rather not be reminded. Ask which approach works best.
- Suggest that your relative tells family and friends; that way they will know not to smoke in your relative's presence and, hopefully, won't tease about trying to give up.

Exercise

Celia, an occupational therapist

'Add years to your life by adding life to your years – participate in exercise you enjoy.'

Exercise is good news for everyone, even for people who have heart problems. The heart is a muscle and, like all muscles, its action can be strengthened by exercise and its blood supply increased. A heart 'trained' by exercise pumps more blood with each beat, so it doesn't have to beat so fast to move the same amount of blood. In the past, treatment for people who suffered heart attacks meant long periods of inactivity and bed rest to allow the heart to heal. This is no longer thought to be necessary: patients are now encouraged to get out of bed and move around very soon after the attack, and are usually offered a rehabilitation programme before discharge.

Information in a book can only be written in a general way, so before taking any form of exercise, all people with a heart problem must check with their doctor first and be sure they understand the type and level of exercise that is suitable for them. As a carer you can help your relative to plan their exercise sensibly, perhaps with the advice of a physiotherapist who is skilled at helping people get the best from an exercise programme. You could join in – shared exercise is much more pleasurable than slogging it out alone.

Why is exercise good for us?

It is never too late to derive some benefit from exercise, and the advantages are well proven. Exercise helps lower blood pressure and improves physical strength, mobility and mental well-being. Physical activity protects the body by maintaining smooth movement in the joints, by strengthening bones and by increasing the efficiency of the heart muscle. It can help to prevent osteoporosis and further heart problems. The Health Development Agency, a government-funded organisation, recommends daily exercise that is energetic enough to make you feel puffed; this level is more than 'merely being busy'. Nevertheless, lighter, less frequent exercise is also beneficial.

It's good to assess the exercise benefits of everything your relative does so that daily activities such as gardening, housework, climbing the stairs and walking to the shops are included in their overall fitness plan. Encourage them to put a bit of vigour into daily living and plan extra activities at least three times a week. Exercise is very good for reducing stress, because it boosts the hormones that produce feelings of happiness and the movement gently relaxes muscle tension.

The message from the experts promotes the three **S**s – stamina, strength and suppleness – as the key elements in keeping fit:

- **Stamina** increases the ability to keep going without getting breathless or suffering from aching muscles.
- **Strength** helps the body to put extra effort into pushing, pulling and lifting safely and without too much difficulty.
- **Suppleness** allows your body to bend, twist and stretch without strain and discomfort.

Ring the changes to prevent boredom

John

'I wish someone had encouraged me to exercise earlier – I thought it was for fitness freaks but cycling has made me feel great.'

When planning an exercise programme choose a range of activities that really get the body moving; variety means you and your relative can choose according to mood and the weather without becoming bored. Exercise should be pleasant and fun, not stressful and competitive. Set achievable aims because, if the effort feels too great, you may both lose enthusiasm. All exercise is safer if muscles are given time to warm up and cool down before and after the main exertion; athletes spend time doing special actions that stretch muscles and increase the heart rate. It's not necessary to learn specific warm up and cool down routines for any of the leisure activities listed below but 'start and finish slowly' is a simple rule that can be applied to all basic types of exercise. The following activities will help you and your relative become fitter without being too strenuous and are all classed as leisure hobbies rather than exercises for fitness fanatics; some can be done alone, some need a partner. If you would like to join a club, look in the *Yellow Pages* or ask for details at the local library.

Walking is a good choice if you have both been inactive recently, because it boosts stamina and allows fitness to build up at a steady rate. It can be done anywhere, needs no special equipment and is free, relaxing and pleasurable if shared with a companion. A beginner should aim to walk one mile in 20–30 minutes, increasing the pace and distance over a few weeks. For sensible preparation and finish, start walking at a slow pace and increase speed and exertion until you are walking briskly; gradually slow down as you approach the end of the walk, and when you reach home give your muscles a gentle stretch before you sit down.

Swimming is a good exercise for people of all ages, because it combines stamina, strength and suppleness. It is often described as the ideal activity, and it's a great stress reducer – and especially good for people who are overweight or have joint or back problems, because the water supports the body. Many people live within reasonable distance of a swimming pool and the charges are often reduced for certain groups of people.

Cycling is another good exercise to improve on the three Ss. It's recommended for people who are overweight and helps reduce stress, as well as being particularly pleasurable. Cycling in the fresh air is the best choice but an indoor cycle machine provides an alternative way to get pedalling (you can pedal while reading a book or watching TV).

Gardening is a wonderfully relaxing way to combine exercise with fresh air and do lots of bending and stretching. Recent research into horticulture therapy has shown it to be very beneficial for people affected by depression.

Golf helps build up stamina and strength, provides fresh air and an opportunity to make new friends. If you have never played golf before, you will be pleasantly surprised at how energising it can be. Enjoy the scenery and don't overdo the sustenance offered at the nineteenth hole!

Bowling is low on stamina and strength but excellent for suppleness and relaxation. Join a club to get the best advantage from indoor and grass bowls, and try the ten pin variety for some challenging fun.

Badminton is a fun game that suits all ages as long as you are matched with someone of similar ability. Join a club to get some tuition and don't be too competitive. Build up skills at a pace that is comfortable. It's quite a vigorous sport that can be played at a range of speeds from gentle to fast and furious, so your relative should check with the doctor before starting this type of exercise.

Exercise and dance classes are readily available in most areas. Ask at a leisure centre about classes to suit your relative's age and ability level. Both types of activity are good for stamina, strength and suppleness, and dancing is especially relaxing and enjoyable.

Yoga is an excellent form of exercise to control movements and breathing and to encourage muscle relaxation. It's good for suppleness and strengthens body muscles but there is not much benefit for stamina, so if your relative gets hooked on yoga, combine it with another exercise that helps to strengthen the heart muscle as well.

Exercising safely

Exercise takes many forms, so be sure to choose activities that give the best physical results combined with lots of pleasure. No one will suggest that your relative takes up exhausting forms of exercise such as hard jogging or squash. Before starting any form of exercise, it is vital that they get permission from their doctor, and are aware of a few safely rules:

- Start the regimen gradually and build up the exertion at a rate that feels comfortable; this is not training for the Olympics!
- Don't exercise for at least two hours after a meal, because the digestive system places an automatic demand on the blood supply to digest the food.
- Wear clothing that is loose and comfortable, shoes or trainers that provide adequate support, and use appropriate equipment when necessary.
- Muscles need to warm up and cool down before and after exercise, so never rush straight into the most strenuous part of the activity; start and stop at a gentle pace.
- Drink plenty of fluids, but not alcohol because this increases dehydration.
- Stop immediately if there are any signs of breathlessness, chest pains or feeling unwell in any way. If exercise has caused problems, however minor, inform the doctor before continuing with the programme.

Leg cramps

Even mild increases in exercise may cause leg cramps for people who have peripheral vascular disease (see page 10), a condition in which the blood supply to the legs is restricted because of 'hardening' and 'furring up' of the arteries. The extra oxygen needed by the muscles cannot be supplied and causes sharp pains, particularly in the calf muscles, that cease as soon as the person takes a rest. In severe cases the pains are brought on after walking only short distances on flat ground. Your relative's doctor will advise about taking exercise if leg cramps are painful.

Sleeping well

Tension and stress are common causes of sleep problems, causing early waking or difficulty dropping off when thoughts race around the brain. If stress is making you or your relative sleep badly, don't rush for medication. Instead, try practising the relaxation techniques described in Chapter 6. Be aware too that many older people naturally take longer to fall asleep, are more likely to wake during the night, and tend to wake earlier in the morning. However, early waking is also a symptom of depression, which may benefit from treatment.

Tips to help settle at night

- Go to bed at a regular time, with a regular routine.
- Make everything as cosy as possible – warm room and comfortable bed.
- Don't eat a big meal late in the day.
- Avoid drinks that contain alcohol or caffeine later in the day, and choose a milky drink at bedtime.
- Cut back on evening fluids if a full bladder is the cause of waking.
- Read or listen to the radio until you naturally feel sleepy. If you wake in the night, do the same or get up and watch some television and repeat the milky drink with a biscuit if you are feeling hungry – don't lie tossing and turning.
- Take regular exercise, but don't be too strenuous late in the day as this type of exercise releases hormones that are stimulating.

Sexual relationships

When to resume sexual relationships after a heart attack or surgery, or how great the risks are for someone who has angina, are questions that many people avoid asking because of embarrassment. Your relative's doctor will be able to reassure them about their condition and will not be embarrassed to discuss the matter. Generally, the advice to people with heart conditions is to treat sex like any other type of exercise. Regular sexual activity that induces slight breathlessness is good news: it aids recovery by strengthening the heart muscle, relieves stress and adds to the feeling of well-being. Normal sex with a known partner puts a strain on the heart equivalent to climbing two flights of stairs!

In the rare cases where sexual activity has brought on a heart attack, there are usually other factors that contributed to the situation. A heavy meal or too much alcohol, and the excitement of having sex with a new partner or unknown person can all put additional strain on the heart. Like any other form of exercise, it's wise to take note of how the body feels: if sexual activity causes discomfort or chest pains, stop immediately and talk to the doctor about the problem.

Impotence

Peripheral vascular disease (see page 10), the condition that causes painful cramps while walking, can also affect sexual performance in some men, leading to difficulty achieving or maintaining an erection. Poor blood supply to the penis may be a factor, but other causes – stress, tiredness, side effects from drugs and leaking veins that cannot retain blood in the penis – all affect the quality of an erection. If impotence is a problem for your relative, do encourage him to seek help from a doctor because special drug treatments are available (for example, Viagra and Testosterone). One question that will be asked is whether there is a morning erection, as this information will help the doctor to decide whether there are physical causes. A change in drug treatment or some relaxation therapy may be all that is needed to improve the situation.

Signs of depression

Immediately after an illness or operation, the time is filled with rest and treatment. However, as your relative recovers, the problem of boredom may become apparent. It's well worth giving this period some thought because, although having time to think about the past and the future will help in adjusting to the change, it is important not to let a state of depression develop, brought on by apathy or feelings of uselessness. Some signs of minor depression – for example, weeping and being withdrawn – are common after a serious illness, but, if you feel that these signs are getting worse, do encourage your relative to seek help from the doctor before it becomes difficult to manage. Talking and listening are excellent ways of starting self-help treatment.

Relieving boredom

Elsie

'Tom was fine at first but I kept finding him staring into space. My daughter helped by suggesting we joined a club together.'

There are many ways to lift the spirit and relieve the boredom. Talk to your relative about the kinds of activity and company they would or would not enjoy. Get out of the house as soon as it is practicable to have a change of scene and overcome early fears about leaving a safe place. Enlist the help of family and friends for all manner of support – from shoppers and drivers to companions and listeners – but try to be aware of how your relative feels, because you may need to act as gate-keeper if too many people want to help.

The public library is the best source of information: most branches carry a wide range of details about local services, with some specialist facilities targeted at carers. As well as books of all sorts, look out for:

- lists of clubs and hobby groups;
- audio and videotapes;
- mobile and doorstep library services for home delivery of books and tapes to people who have difficulty getting to a library because of illness, disability or caring responsibilities;
- 'Talking News' style services providing a range of interesting items via postal tapes – usually for visually impaired people but often extended to people with other disabilities;

- 'befrienders' schemes where volunteers come to the house to chat or play games with people who are temporarily or permanently housebound; and
- branches of University of the Third Age (U3A) that offer a vast range of daytime study and recreational classes for older people who wish to keep their minds stimulated (national address on page 190).

Margaret and Jim

'We thoroughly enjoyed the art class. It was a good start for us, providing a gentle interest and a new group of friends.'

Transport

As recovery continues, you and your relative may want to venture further away from home, perhaps for a shopping trip or a hospital appointment, but this can present travel problems if driving is restricted or not comfortable. Schemes are available in most areas, run by local authorities and voluntary organisations, providing transport for older and disabled people, with their carers as escorts. The journey is usually free or subsidised, depending on personal circumstances.

The main schemes that help people with transport are:

- **Dial-a-ride and community transport schemes** provide door-to-door service for shopping or similar local outings for people who cannot use public transport (see national address for the Community Transport Association on page 181 or ask at the local authority, volunteer bureau or library). They use converted cars, or minibuses with tail-lifts and ramps.
- **Social car schemes** are available in many parts of the country, especially rural areas, for use by people who do not have access to a vehicle and find using public transport difficult. Typical journeys cover surgery and hospital appointments, chiropody care, shopping

69

trips, lunch club meetings and visits to friends and relatives. They are locally based and independently operated (usually by a group of volunteers) and should not be confused with hospital car schemes, which can be accessed only through health services.

- **Hospital car schemes/medical patient transport services** are usually run by the ambulance service and arranged through GPs' surgeries. They are available only for people who have a medical condition and cannot get to the hospital independently; one companion is usually allowed.

- **The Blue Badge Parking Scheme** (previously known as the Orange Badge Scheme) provides a national arrangement of parking concessions for people with severe walking difficulties who travel as drivers or passengers. Badge holders are exempt from certain parking restrictions, including free parking at on-street parking meters and for up to two hours on single and double yellow lines in England, Wales and Northern Ireland (or without any time limit in Scotland). Badges are issued through social services departments. Check local rules carefully as some London Boroughs do not offer free parking arrangements.

- **Motability** is a charity set up to help disabled people who want to spend the higher mobility component of their Disability Living Allowance (DLA) or War Pensioner's Mobility Supplement on a car, scooter or wheelchair (see address on page 186). Vehicles may be purchased or leased, and help may be available with the cost of special adaptations. A relative, friend or carer may apply and drive on behalf of a disabled person. There is no mobility component attached to Attendance Allowance (the DLA equivalent awarded to people aged 65 and over).

- **The Disabled Persons Railcard** gives up to one third off a range of rail tickets. An application form and booklet called *Rail Travel for Disabled Passengers* can be obtained from main stations or from the national address on page 183. Train companies can provide special arrangements for disabled passengers, but they must be given a minimum of 24 hours' notice before the journey.

- **Shopmobility** schemes provide free wheelchair/scooter loan services in many town centres for anyone with a mobility problem.

Users can usually park free or be met at the bus station or taxi rank by prior arrangement. An escort service is often available for people who are visually impaired or wheelchair users.

■ **Taxicard** (or similar name) is a service providing subsidised taxi fares; it is run by some larger councils for disabled people who are unable to use public transport. One passenger may accompany the cardholder. Ask at your local council office.

■ **The Disability Living Allowance Unit** (address on page 182) provides information about exemption from road tax for vehicles used exclusively by or for disabled people receiving the higher rate of the mobility component of Disability Living Allowance (DLA) or War Pensioner's Mobility Supplement.

Holidays

Joan

'We always planned our holiday so that I felt comfortable knowing how to reach a doctor. I kept the telephone numbers handy.'

Once your relative is feeling better, you may all benefit from a holiday. The GP will advise you about when the time is right and explain the main aspects of your relative's health care, especially if you are going abroad. At the planning stage it would be wise to find out about the following points in case you need to make special arrangements for:

■ taking drugs out of the country;

■ insurance cover because your relative has an existing illness; or

■ dealing with the effects of heat and sunlight (or opt for somewhere with a cooler climate).

Holiday planning services that specifically deal with information for older or disabled people can be used, and this may reduce much of the load on you. The organisations listed below are selected from the many that provide help:

- **Tripscope** offers a nationwide travel and transport information and advice service for older and disabled people (address on page 189).
- **The Holiday Care Service** provides information and advice on holidays, travel facilities and respite care for people with disabilities, on low income or with special needs (address on page 184). A reservation helpline and holiday insurance information for disabled people are also available.
- **RADAR (Royal Association for Disability and Rehabilitation)** campaigns to empower disabled people; produces some guides including a holiday guide for disabled people.
- The website **www.everybody.co.uk** provides information on services offered to people with disabilities by 50 major airlines. It also lists hotels in the UK that are accessible.
- **The Special Families Home Swap Register** produces a quarterly register to enable physically disabled people to swap their home for breaks elsewhere in the country (address on page 188). The homes listed are suitably equipped to accommodate people with physical disabilities. A small fee is charged for registration but there are no other costs: accommodation is free.
- **The Winged Fellowship** provides respite care and holidays for physically disabled people, with or without a partner, in purpose-built holiday centres and on overseas and touring holidays (address on page 190). Trained staff and volunteers provide care.

Conclusion

Celia, an occupational therapist

'Having a heart attack results in many changes – rise to the challenge!'

This chapter has encouraged you to focus on some of the inevitable changes that are taking place for you and your relative, and has offered some hints about how to accept the changes and move forward.

Adjusting to a new situation is never straightforward, and it can be very stressful if the event that triggered the change was upsetting and beyond your control. We all deal with problems better if we feel that there is an element of choice involved and if we can retain some control over the situation. After a while the memory of unpleasant events will fade and you and your relative will be able to move forward with confidence and benefit from changes in lifestyle. Chapter 6 provides an insight into causes of stress and offers some techniques to help you both cope while you adjust.

For more information

ⓘ Age Concern Factsheets (see page 197 for details of how to obtain factsheets):
26 *Travel Information for Older People*
45 *Staying Healthy in Later Life*

ⓘ *Intimate Relations: Living and Loving in Later Life*, published by Age Concern Books (see page 194 for details).

ⓘ Age Concern Information Sheet IS6 *Holidays for Older People*.

4 How to cope with failing health

However well you care for your relative, their heart disease may begin to get worse. It is never possible to make forecasts about how an illness will develop or how long each stage will last but if the person is older it is inevitable that their health will eventually fail. You may wish to deal with the emotional side of this knowledge alone or ask for support, but many of the practical difficulties will be the same for all carers.

This chapter provides information to help you make early plans that will make life easier further along the road. It may seem difficult and even wrong to start thinking about failing health before that time has come but many families say it's less stressful to make decisions and deal with events if they have had time to think about the future and come to terms with changing circumstances.

Caring for an ill person at home can be a difficult undertaking and usually creates a mixture of emotions. Carers experience tremendous reward coupled with extreme tiredness; they feel anxiety and sadness and frequently become frustrated at the inadequacies of the 'system'. Despite this range of hurdles it is possible to overcome the practical problems and most carers feel determined to provide quality care at home for as long as possible.

This chapter explains about heart failure, and how it is diagnosed and treated. It examines the support services which may be available to you locally and discusses the different care options which you may have to consider. There are no right or wrong decisions, nor are there effortless ways of dealing with the position – simply do the best you can.

What is heart failure?

'Heart failure' is the name given to the characteristic signs and symptoms that develop when the heart is damaged and can no longer pump blood around the body in sufficient quantities to keep the organs working normally. The most noticeable effects are:

- loss of energy;
- tiredness after moderate exercise or even at rest;
- severe breathlessness; and
- swelling of the ankles, feet and abdomen.

The heart can be damaged by a number of diseases, the most common of which is narrowing of the coronary arteries that supply oxygen and other nutrients to the heart muscle. In severe cases this can lead to a heart attack and affect the pumping action of the heart. As the performance of the heart deteriorates, blood pressure falls, the blood vessels narrow and the kidneys automatically retain fluids in the body to try to maintain the blood pressure level. This is a difficult balance to achieve and often an over-correction occurs: too much water floods the system and leaks out of the blood vessels into the tissues, causing the characteristic swelling of the feet, ankles and abdomen, and tissues over the base of the spine in someone who sits or lies rather than being mobile and walking about. Extra fluid builds up in the lungs, making breathing difficult. At first this is noticeable only during exercise but, as the heart grows weaker, the breathing is affected at rest – even in bed. In some cases the breathlessness is aggravated by a cough. In addition, the constriction of small blood vessels leads to an insufficient blood supply to the kidneys and other organs, reducing their ability to function satisfactorily.

It is unlikely that heart failure will occur immediately after a heart attack, because the heart is amazingly strong. Over the years, however, its performance weakens and heart failure comes on gradually. This gradual deterioration can also occur with other heart problems, such as heart muscle failure (cardiomyopathy), continual high blood pressure or valvular heart disease. Once the efficiency of the heart has started to fail, the process tends to speed up with the severity of the disease.

Diagnosis

In order to make a diagnosis the doctor will take a medical history to find out about any previous heart problems and other illnesses that give similar signs and symptoms. Breathlessness is common in people who have respiratory problems (for example, because they smoke heavily), who are obese or who have severe anaemia; and ankle swelling is a symptom of varicose veins (see page 8).

The doctor will make a physical examination to estimate whether the heart is enlarged; look for signs of blood congestion in the veins of the neck; check the heart rate and rhythm; and listen to how the heart sounds. Tests that confirm the diagnosis include:

- an electrocardiogram (ECG) (see page 15);
- an ultrasound scan (see page 16);
- an echo-cardiogram – a painless test that gives visual pictures of the heart in action; and
- a chest X-ray to show the size and position of the heart.

Treatment has a much better effect if the problem is diagnosed early and your relative adapts to a slower pace of life, causing less strain on the heart.

Treatment

Doctors will plan treatment for heart failure by investigating the original problem. If it is caused by high blood pressure, thyroid gland problems or faulty heart valves, the symptoms can be improved with medication or surgery, or a combination of both. Unfortunately, not all forms of heart failure can be prevented or cured, because the deterioration often cannot be reversed. For example, any narrowing of the arteries that has already occurred in coronary heart disease cannot be changed; once the heart begins to fail, no further treatment of the arteries will help. However, the outlook is not entirely bleak, because treatments for heart failure have improved considerably over the years. As discussed in Chapters 1 and 3, symptoms can be relieved through medication and changes in lifestyle – the most important are stopping smoking, improving the diet, taking moderate exercise and reducing excess weight. Your relative's doctor will recommend and explain any changes that will help the problem.

Medication is the most common treatment used to improve the performance of the heart and ease the unpleasant symptoms. Most people with heart failure are treated using a combination of drugs. These may include:

- **digoxin** (digitalis) to steady and strengthen the heartbeat;
- **vasodilators** (ACE inhibitors) to improve the flow of blood through the blood vessels;
- **diuretics** (water tablets) to increase the output of urine, in order to reduce swelling in the tissues and thus improve breathlessness and pressure from swollen ankles; and/or
- **beta blockers** to slow down and lower the force of the heartbeat. This category of drug, once contra-indicated in the treatment of heart failure, is now known to be beneficial when given to carefully selected patients. If this drug is prescribed to your relative their doctor will wish to observe their progress closely.

If heart failure does not respond to medical treatment in a younger patient, the possibility of a heart transplant (cardiac transplantation) can be considered.

Problems arising from treatment

Everyone taking medication for heart failure receives regular check-ups because drug treatment carries risks of side (unwanted) effects. The most common side effects are related to too little potassium in the bloodstream from excess water loss due to the water tablets and the effects of the ACE inhibitors. Loss of potassium leads to tiredness and an irregular heartbeat. Excess digoxin can build up in the body, causing nausea and a slow pulse rate. Finally, the vasodilators can lower the blood pressure too much, causing some dizziness.

If the doctor suspects that medication is causing unwanted side effects, blood tests can be done to check the drug levels in the system. If you or your relative have any concerns about possible side effects of treatment, do discuss this with the doctor promptly, because it can take a while to stabilise treatments and the state of the heart itself may alter. If the problems remain untreated or changes in symptoms develop, the heart failure will continue to get worse, resulting in quite marked distress. But *never* stop any medication without speaking to the doctor first.

For more information

ⓘ *Management of Heart Failure: Understanding NICE Guidance – Information for People with Heart Failure, their Carers, and the Public*, published by the National Institute for Clinical Excellence. Available from the NHS Response Line, tel: 0870 1555 455, quoting reference number N0248, or the NICE website at www.nice.org.uk

Local support services

Melly, a community nurse

'If you are unsure about caring, speak to your community (district) nurse. We know all about local services and you don't always have to get the doctor to refer you.'

Although you may have been caring for a while, it is possible that you are not familiar with the full range of local services. Why not find out now what help is available, before pressure builds up and you reach crisis point. Community nurses (called district nurses in some areas) or social workers are thought by many people to be a last point of call when a crisis has arisen, but they can give support and advice to carers long before that stage is reached. The assessment process and how it can help you and your relative is the key to all types of care and is open to anyone who feels they are in need of a support service. Getting extra help does not mean that you have failed or that you are receiving charity. You may be eligible for help with, for example, personal care, practical support and respite care. Ask at your GP's surgery, health centre or social services office.

Look at the checklist below. If you answer 'yes' to any of the questions and would like further information, you should ask for help locally.

- Have you just started to care for someone else?
- Do you think the person you care for should have an assessment or re-assessment of their needs?
- Do you want to talk to someone about how you feel and what help you are entitled to receive?
- Would you like to know more about respite care facilities?
- Do you feel exhausted and close to breaking point?
- Do you need help to move your relative safely – for both of your sakes?
- Do you think extra equipment would help you to manage better?
- Do you feel that you could have received a better quality service or better support from those providing care?

Joan

'Someone showed me a book about services for carers after Peter had died. I had never realised that there were so many organisations that provide help and support.'

Support for you as a carer and for your relative is available locally from a number of sources run by statutory, private and voluntary organisa-tions. Most of these services can be accessed via the NHS or the social services department, and your relative will be assessed as requiring 'nursing' care or 'personal' care. There may seem to be little difference in practical terms, and in reality the services try to work very closely together. However, it does make a difference to the way that the need for care is assessed and how care is paid for.

A National Service Framework for Older People was launched in 2001. It is a 10-year programme to improve the health and social care of older people, whether they are being cared for at home, in a care home or in hospital. It requires health and social services to work more closely to offer a seamless service to older people, and has eight standards to be addressed when they are making decisions about care requirements.

Many agencies use contract workers but all care is regulated by the Commission for Social Care Inspection (CSCI) (previously the National Care Standards Commission), under the Care Standards Act (England) 2000 and Regulations of Care (Scotland) 2001, or the Commission for Healthcare Audit and Inspection (CHAI).

Since April 2002, the manner in which charges are calculated for home care in the separate UK countries differs slightly. Guidelines giving the appropriate charging structures are available locally: ask the social services department for information.

Social services

Penny, a carers' support worker

'Unfortunately, there are gaps in services. Carers must ask for a proper face-to-face assessment; give only basic details over the telephone.'

Janet, a carers' support worker

'Ask questions that are important for you and your relative. Don't rely on guesswork, as situations and availability of services do change. Use paper to jot down headings of things you want to discuss before you meet a professional person.'

Local social services departments are the main agencies for co-ordinating the provision of community care services for older people. They should be listed in the telephone directory under the name of the local authority. Not all people with heart problems will require direct services from a social services department, so skip over this section if you feel it does not apply to your relative's needs at present. The information will be helpful for some families at some times. In all areas close liaison takes place between community nurses and social workers, and care will be shared when necessary.

Assessments

Janet, a carers' support worker

'Many services have been reduced in areas where budgets are tight. Carers have a legal right to a proper assessment; this is not affected by cutbacks.'

Rani, social worker

'As a professional person working directly with families of older people, I acknowledge and respect the fact that not everyone is cut out to be a "carer". I meet many families who express feelings of limitation and I support them to find an alternative solution.'

Social services departments are responsible for providing a wide range of home, residential and day care services. This is provided direct through their own home care service, or purchased for your relative from voluntary or commercial organisations (sometimes called the independent sector). Demand for services is heavy and most departments have limited financial resources, so they apply strict eligibility criteria (tests) to decide which services to provide.

The local authority has a duty to assess anyone who it might have to provide a service for. Assessment – or care assessment – is a term used to describe how they find out what sort of help and support someone needs. The Government has introduced a Single Assessment

Process for Older People (SAP) which is intended to integrate assessments for social care and other health needs. This should save you from having to give basic information more than once.

These assessments, in some form, apply generally throughout the UK, although there are some local variations. You can find out how assessment works in your relative's local authority by asking to see a copy of its long-term care charter called *Better Care, Higher Standards* (see page 39). The example of assessment given below is typical, although the availability of individual services will differ from area to area.

The SAP guidance suggests four types of assessment: contact; overview; specialist; and comprehensive. Which type of assessment is appropriate will depend upon the nature and complexity of your relative's needs. A contact assessment might involve the gathering of basic information and identification of significant needs. An overview assessment is more wide-ranging and explores needs in the context of some or all of the 'domains' or subject areas set out in government guidance called *Fair Access to Care Services*. These domains are:

- user's perspective;
- clinical background;
- disease prevention;
- personal care and physical well-being;
- senses;
- mental health;
- relationships;
- safety and immediate environment; and
- resources.

A specialist assessment might be a detailed examination of a particular need. A comprehensive assessment is an in-depth assessment which might be appropriate where an overview assessment will not suffice. Your relative's ability to live independently is an important consideration, both currently and also in the future if your relative's needs are not met.

After the assessment, the local authority will decide whether or not it should provide or arrange community care services for your relative under its eligibility criteria. Once it is decided that a person is eligible to receive services, it will then usually carry out a financial assessment to establish how much they should contribute towards the cost of those services. Discussions should take place between everyone immediately involved to devise a 'care plan'. Your relative should be given a copy of the written record of the care plan, which should include a date on which the plan will be reviewed.

Each local authority has discretion about whether it will charge people for community care services, depending on personal circumstances. In Scotland personal care is free for people aged 65 and over, but your relative will still be charged for non-personal care services. In England and Wales if the care comes under the definition of 'Intermediate care' (ie to avoid your relative going to hospital or when they have just come out of hospital), it will be free for six weeks. In Scotland people get free services for six weeks when they come out of hospital (even if some of the care is non-personal care). Any charge your relative does pay must be 'reasonable' for them to pay and based only on their resources. Your relative has the right to ask the local authority to reduce the amount or waive it altogether.

The eligibility criteria continue to apply if your relative is already receiving services. The needs of you both will be reassessed by means of a review and services may change as a result of this process. Again, everyone immediately concerned should be fully involved and informed of any decisions about future care.

If your relative does not agree with the result of the assessment, or the charges, they can appeal against it using the social services complaints procedure (a social worker or care manager will advise you about the process). Social services departments will investigate any complaint seriously and will suggest that you obtain independent advice. The local Citizens Advice Bureau may be able to advise you.

For more information

i Age Concern Factsheet 41 *Local Authority Assessment for Community Care Services* (see page 197 for details of how to obtain factsheets).

Community care services

Help for adults with day-to-day care, living in their own homes, includes:

- personal care (eg washing, toileting, going to bed);
- practical help (eg housework or shopping), although this type of help is more likely to be provided by a separate agency;
- support for carers who may be partners, relatives or friends (eg respite care);
- advice and equipment from an occupational therapist (eg commodes, bed raisers); and
- help for people with specialist needs from skilled staff (eg those with hearing or sight loss, or physical disabilities).

Care assistants give personal care, such as washing and toileting, and carry out basic treatments. They are not trained nurses and so do not carry out elaborate nursing procedures.

Health care services (NHS)

Services from the NHS for people with health care needs include:

- the provision of general and specialist care;
- loan of equipment;
- rehabilitation;
- respite health care; and
- continuing NHS care (ie, where the NHS pays the full fees for agreed nursing care).

The main decisions about what health services will be provided for people locally are taken by Primary Care Trusts, which also commission services from other NHS Trusts and the independent sector, to complement their own provision. You can get information about health services from your GP surgery or health centres, or from NHS Direct (Tel: 0845 46 47). NHS and social services staff should work closely with your GP to maintain continuity of care.

Local health services tend to fall into three categories:

■ **Acute health care** Given at NHS Hospital Trusts that offer special-ist tests and treatments through inpatient and outpatient services.

■ **Community health care** Provided by NHS Primary Care Trusts that offer day-to-day care from a range of services, including com-munity psychiatric and general nursing, physiotherapy, occupational therapy and chiropody.

■ **Tertiary health care** Provided by care homes.

Eligibility criteria for continuing NHS health care

Each NHS Trust sets its eligibility criteria for these services based on national guidelines. They must be published and should be available from the local NHS body. Your relative's health care needs will be assessed against these criteria. An NHS patient receiving treatment in hospital and requiring services after discharge will be assessed before leaving hospital. If long-term, hospital-based care is not needed, social services and NHS professionals will work together to prepare a care plan to be provided in the person's own home or in a care home. The care given to each patient is overseen by one senior person, who works with a small team of staff to ensure consistent care. The name given to this key person may vary from area to area, but it is designed to fulfil the same purpose – the role of care 'manager'.

The views and wishes of the person and their family are taken into account. If they do not agree with the decision to discharge the patient from hospi-tal they can ask an independent review panel to look at the decision. If this applies to you, the Patient Advice and Liaison Service (PALS) in England, the Community Health Councils in Wales or the Health Council in Scotland can help you if you are unsure how to proceed (see pages 93–94).

Home care (NHS)

The Community Nursing Service operates throughout the country, pro-viding general and psychiatric nursing treatment and care for people who remain at home. Community general and mental health nurses are often based at GP surgeries and health centres; patients are usually referred by their GPs but anyone can contact a community nurse direct. If a care plan has already been set up following hospital discharge, the appropriate community nurse will call automatically. But if your relative has not been discharged recently and you feel you need help or advice, you may telephone for an assessment.

Don't wait until you are desperate, particularly if the state of your relative's health is failing quickly or they have become incontinent. Community nurses can provide a great deal of local information about resources and can put you in touch with other services and arrange equipment and items such as continence pads. Ask for a telephone number at your surgery or leave a message for the nurse.

For more information

ⓘ Age Concern Factsheets (see page 197 for details of how to obtain factsheets):
20 *NHS Continuing Care, NHS Funded Registered Nursing Care and Intermediate Care*
37 *Hospital Discharge Arrangements, and NHS Continuing Health Care Services*
44 *NHS Services and Older People.*

ⓘ Contact **NHS Direct** on 0845 46 47.

General Practitioner

A General Practitioner (GP) is the community doctor based at the local health centre or surgery. You might also hear your GP being called a Primary Health Care Practitioner. The GP is the key figure that your relative should visit first and, depending on the severity of the problem, they are able to deal with most aspects of general illnesses – from diagnosis to treatment. The majority of care given by GPs is arranged through the local surgery or health centre and the GP is the person who would refer your relative to other health care services.

Eric, a GP

'The surgery is often the first place to ask for help. Keep "knocking on the door", as you sometimes need to get your GP to understand what you want. GPs should be a signpost to other services, and if you need a home visit make this clear.'

Pharmacists (chemists) and prescriptions

Pharmacists in local chemist shops provide a number of services to the community and are a valuable source of information about medicines, 'over-the-counter' treatments (which don't need a prescription) and any minor health problems that are not serious enough to take to a surgery. Pharmacists will advise you to speak to the GP if they feel there is a need for medical treatment. Before you speak to a pharmacist, make a list of all medication being taken by your relative so that he or she can be sure that drugs will not interact with each other.

In particular, a pharmacist is responsible for making up prescriptions for medicines or certain medical aids. You may take a prescription to any pharmacy but, for people living in rural areas, a dispensing service is available at surgeries and health centres if the nearest pharmacist/ chemist shop is more than one mile away; ask about the availability of this service if you are unsure. There is normally a charge for prescriptions, but certain categories of people qualify for free medication, including: people aged 60 and over, people on certain benefits and people with certain illnesses such as diabetes. Having coronary heart disease does not automatically mean that your relative will be exempt.

Pharmacists can help in other ways, such as supplying and/or filling a special box to help someone take the correct drug dose at the correct time of day, and putting medicines in non-child-proof containers if a person has difficulty opening standard caps.

Pre-payment certificates are available to help spread the cost for people who need regular medication but do not qualify for free prescriptions. Enquire about these or any other pharmacy-related details at your local pharmacist/chemist shop or GP surgery.

Independent care providers

Help is also available from private and voluntary agencies that offer a range of services, including personal and domestic care, residential care, respite facilities, holiday accommodation and companionship. One such organisation, Crossroads – Caring for Carers (see address on

87

page 182), has schemes in most areas of England and Wales. Charges made by independent care providers vary and may be greater than the rates charged by social services.

If you wish to obtain care from an independent agency for your relative, or to top up the amount of care they receive from the local authority, ask your social worker for details or look in *Yellow Pages* or check with a national organisation such as those listed at the back of the book. Some independent agencies belong to organisations that require them to meet certain standards, such as those set by the United Kingdom Home Care Association. UKHCA (address on page 189) has a free leaflet called *Choosing Care in Your Home*. The charity Counsel and Care (address on page 181) has a database of home care agencies. Agencies that provide nurses or care workers who carry out personal care tasks have to be registered with the Commission for Social Care Inspection (national address on page 181) and should be regularly inspected by the Commission to ensure that they comply with minimum standards. These standards include requirements to provide detailed information about the services that they provide and to have written contracts with users.

Your relative can purchase all their care needs from private agencies (if they are willing to pay the charge). Local authorities are required to offer 'direct payments' (ie money to arrange their own services) to older people who need a service and who meet certain criteria. (Nursing care is free in any setting in England, and nursing and personal care costs are free in Scotland.)

For more information

ℹ️ Age Concern Factsheets (see page 197 for details of how to obtain factsheets):
6 *Finding Help at Home*
24 *Direct Payments from Social Services*
46 *Paying for Care and Support at Home.*

ℹ️ Contact the **Independent Healthcare Association** at the address on page 185.

ℹ️ Contact the **United Kingdom Home Care Association** (UKHCA) at the address on page 189.

Care homes

Christine

'My father went into a home and he was given good care. But we visited several homes before we found one that he felt was right for him.'

Care homes offer permanent accommodation to people who are unable to live independently in the community. This includes disabled people and frail older people, including those with dementia. Many homes also offer respite care facilities and other temporary places.

All residential and nursing homes are now called 'care homes' (following the implementation of Care Standards Act (England) 2000 and Regulations of Care (Scotland) 2001). The new procedures started in 2002, with different categories of home available, depending on the types of care offered. Various combinations of care might be offered; for example:

- homes that offer personal care only;
- homes that offer additional nursing care;
- homes that offer personal and nursing care with the facility to provide medicines and medical treatments; or
- homes that also cater for people with dementia and those who are terminally ill.

At the outset of caring you and your relative may be coping well and may not wish to consider a care home as an option. However, over a period of time, if the care situation becomes stressed or your relative's health deteriorates, moving into a care home may become the best or only choice open to you both. In such a situation, it's vital that everyone involved in the decision has a chance to express their feelings about seeking permanent care, provided they are mentally capable. If your relative is able, you should discuss with them the merits of staying at home or entering a care home, and weigh up the possible advantages and disadvantages for everyone concerned. Think about all the factors that might influence the final decision, including:

89

- the benefit of increased safety and care provided by trained staff;
- peace of mind and less stress for the carer, especially if relationships have become strained;
- ready-made companionship – but loss of privacy and independence;
- feelings of guilt and the loss of a close relative from the immediate family circle;
- the costs of travel and time;
- the difficulty in finding a suitable home;
- the overall cost of residential care set against charges for care at home (include Attendance Allowance in your calculations for care at home – see page 114); and
- whether it is possible for your relative to continue to live at home or in retirement (sheltered) or 'extra care' housing if the level of services were increased?

Choosing a care home

It is not easy to decide which type of home to live in and the decision should not be made hurriedly. A list of addresses can be obtained from the local authority, and details can then be obtained direct from the individual homes.

Gill

'As my husband's illness got worse, we had a family conference about what would be the best thing to do. We all wanted to keep him at home with us.'

Ask around among your friends and acquaintances about the care homes you are considering. Word of mouth is often a useful source of information and a measure of local feeling. When your relative is getting closer to making a decision, gather together local details, draw up a shortlist and arrange to visit the homes. It's important to get a feel for the atmosphere and the care provided. If possible, see if you and your relative can visit to share a meal or other activities with the current residents. You might want to ask yourselves some questions to help assess what type of home would be best:

- How mobile is your relative?
- What is your relative's current physical and mental state, and is this likely to change rapidly?
- How much care is needed: round-the-clock cover or daytime support only?
- What type of care is needed: nursing care, including medication and treatments, or just personal hygiene?
- Will special aids and equipment be needed?

Remember also the things that your relative likes to do or feels are important. For example, if being able to attend church, enjoying favourite meals, having regular visitors or playing bridge is important to them, you should try to ensure that they can continue to do so.

Registration and inspection

All care homes, whether independent or statutory, are subject to standard registration and inspection procedures, carried out locally by the Commission for Social Care Inspection (previously the National Care Standards Commission). Care homes should be inspected twice a year and all inspection reports must be publicly available. The Commission should be able to give you details of homes on its register. Some independent agencies belong to organisations that require them to meet their own independent standards, such as those set by the United Kingdom Home Care Association (UKHCA), in addition to the national criteria set by the Care Standards Act.

Paying for care in a care home

If the NHS arranges care for your relative in a home which provides nursing care, they will be regarded as long-stay NHS patients and the NHS will pay in full for their care. In Scotland, personal care as well as nursing care is free. In England and Wales the NHS funds the care provided by a registered nurse in a care home. In England there are three 'bands', depending on the level of nursing your relative is assessed as needing.

If your relative needs help with care home costs, they may be able to get help from the local authority and they may also get benefits from the Department for Work and Pensions. Before the local authority can offer any financial help, your relative will have to have an assessment of their needs (see pages 81–83). If your relative has savings of more than an upper capital limit (£20,000 in England in 2004), your relative will have to pay the full fees of the home until their savings reach that amount. The local authority will also look at your relative's income, including any Pension Credit they receive. Each authority sets limits as to the maximum amount which it will usually pay for a particular type of care. If your relative enters a home costing more, a third party might have to make up the shortfall beween the local authority's limit and the actual cost of the home.

Even if your relative is willing and able to meet the full fees, it is still a good idea to ask for an assessment from social services to help you choose the right sort of home and ensure that all the options are clear. A formal assessment is also important well in advance of a time that financial help is likely to be required if your relative's money is running out.

For more information

ⓘ Age Concern Factsheets (see page 197 for details of how to obtain factsheets):
10 *Local Authority Charging Procedures for Care Homes*
29 *Finding Care Home Accommodation*
38 *Treatment of the Former Home as Capital for People in Care Homes*
39 *Paying for Care in a Care Home if You Have a Partner*
40 *Transfer of Assets and Paying for Care in a Care Home*

ⓘ Contact the **Commission for Social Care Inspection** at the address on page 181.

ⓘ **Counsel and Care** (address on page 181) is a voluntary organisation which can give advice and information about care homes.

ⓘ Contact the **Elderly Accommodation Counsel** at the address on page 183.

Voluntary services

There is a wide range of voluntary organisations that provide services, self-help and support to carers at national and regional levels. Many of these organisations are directly contracted by the NHS and social services to provide care locally. No two areas will offer identical services, so you will have to find out what you can expect to obtain in your area. The two main sources of information about the voluntary sector can be found in the telephone directory under 'Council for Voluntary Services' (CVS) and 'Volunteer Bureau/Centre' (or contact the your local public library which will have a list of local organisations).

Some voluntary organisations only provide services that are broadly targeted – for example, advice and information available from Citizens Advice Bureaux – while others offer help related to specific conditions and illnesses. The latter are most likely to offer support through newsletters and self-help groups. Some services provided by the voluntary sector carry charges to cover costs. In some places the voluntary sector provides a number of local facilities, professionally managed by well-trained staff, which are used on behalf of the community by NHS and social services; day centres and meals on wheels are good examples.

Making a complaint

If you are not happy with the services you receive from any organisation (NHS, social services, the private sector or voluntary agencies), try to resolve the situation as soon as possible by speaking to the person involved – this could be the senior nurse on duty, your care co-ordinator or a manager. If you are still not satisfied and wish to take the matter further, contact a customer relations department or equivalent (a voluntary organisation will have a management committee) and ask for details of their complaints procedure. For independent help with the complaints procedure, contact your local Citizens Advice Bureau or PALS (Patient Advice and Liaison Service). NHS Direct (Tel: 0845 46 47) can tell you how to contact the PALS. The PALS will also be able to tell you about a new service supporting those making a complaint about health services – Independent Complaints Advocacy Services (ICAS), which have replaced Community Health Councils. These provide an advocacy service for people who want to make a formal complaint.

Respite care

> ### *Gill*
>
> 'Having a break was difficult. I felt guilty about leaving my husband, although he said he was fine. He did miss me, but after a break I felt ready to carry on for a bit longer.'

All carers need a break from caring, to be alone or to spend time with other family members and friends. This type of break is called 'respite care' and can take many forms:

- a couple of hours out to do some shopping, read a magazine or visit a friend;
- a longer period to go away on a weekend break or a holiday;
- time spent at home catching up on jobs while your relative goes to a day centre; or
- an uninterrupted night's sleep.

Breaks like these are not a luxury – they are essential for your own health and well-being and will help you to cope better. Your relative might also welcome a break from the usual environment or routine. Everyone needs to 'recharge their batteries' and ease the stressload, so, even if you feel fine at present, try not to leave it until you are desperate for a break before attempting to make arrangements. The Government's NHS Plan recognises the importance of respite care in its *Better Care, Higher Standards* Charter, which indicates that information about 'types of breaks for carers' must be available locally. Respite care can always be organised if there is an emergency, but it's much better to have a regular time set aside that enables you to plan ahead and have something to look forward to. The energy needed to organise a break might be more than you can take on if you are at crisis point.

You might be doubtful about handing the care of your relative over to someone else, even for an hour or so, but remember that the break will be good for both of you. A social worker or community nurse can help you make arrangements or you can contact a national agency, such as the two listed below:

- **The BNA (British Nursing Association)** provides care assistants, 'home helps' and qualified nurses to care for individual people in their own homes. A wide range of services is offered, including convalescent care, night care, personal care, shopping, companionship and respite care. The organisation caters for every level of need from occasional visits to live-in care. Look in the telephone directory for a local number or contact them at the address on page 179.
- **Crossroads – Caring for Carers** schemes are part of a national network set up to provide practical help and support to older and disabled people and their carers. Each situation is assessed individually; the trained care attendant takes over the role of the family carer. Using the Crossroads scheme will give you an opportunity for a respite break at a time of your choosing; care is given 365 days of the year. Look in the telephone directory for a local number or contact them at the address on page 182.

Charges are usually made for respite care; each organisation will give you details according to your relative's circumstances. If regular respite care is part of your relative's care from social services, ask them what charges, if any, there might be. People who meet their health authority's criteria for NHS respite health care may have this provided in a hospital. (There is no charge for respite health care from the NHS.)

Day care

Gill

'The ambulance came once a week to take Bob to the day centre, until his health began to fail. He didn't mind going because he realised that I could go out and have my hair cut and have a break. The social worker set it up for us.'

Day care for your relative is another way for you to have time to yourself, and for your relative to enjoy other activities and different company. All local authorities and many voluntary organisations offer day-care facilities at specially run day centres. Some services are provided in purpose-built day centres, whereas others share accommodation in community centres or care homes. All offer support to carers and older people, and cover a range of needs from social activities and lunch through to specialist care. Your relative can receive chiropody, hairdressing, a bath if this is difficult at home, sit quietly and doze, or chat to staff and other users. The staff are trained care assistants with additional volunteer help in many centres. For more details, ask your social worker or community nurse.

Help with continence

Laura

'The community nurse said that my husband was eligible for incontinence pads and the boxes arrived at the door. The pads made such a difference because I had less washing and my husband slept better because he stopped worrying about wetting the bed.'

If your relative is incontinent, excellent help can be found in most areas through the Continence Advisory Service. Ask at your relative's GP surgery for details. A community nurse or continence adviser will make an assessment. Incontinence has many causes, and it may be possible to improve the symptoms considerably with treatment. For people who have heavy urine and soiling problems, continence pads are available and it may be possible to make use of a home collection laundry service. Facilities vary around the country.

For more information

i Age Concern Factsheet 23 *Help with Continence* (see page 197 for details of how to obtain factsheets).

i **The Continence Foundation** (address on page 181) can provide advice and details of how to contact your local service.

Meals on wheels

A meals service is provided for many older or disabled people. In many areas it is run by the Women's Royal Voluntary Service and other local organisations, and these reasonably priced meals can be delivered either hot daily or as a pre-packed frozen service at regular intervals. Referral is usually via a healthcare professional or the social services department.

Extra equipment

For carers looking after someone at home, further difficulties arise as their relative becomes less mobile. Immobility for people suffering from heart disease tends to develop gradually as their health and strength fail – unlike the abruptness of paralysis immediately following a stroke for example – so for you and your relative each stage can be assessed and you can adjust to whatever degree of movement remains. Aids and equipment to help with moving and handling patients are used frequently by professional carers nowadays, as part of Health and Safety regulations. Useful pieces of equipment to ask about are:

■ **Wheelchair** The effort required to walk even short distances may create unnecessary isolation, especially if breathing is difficult, so for mobility inside and outside the house a wheelchair is essential.

- **Urine bottle/bedpan** Many people prefer to purchase these items from a pharmacist/chemist shop, but bedpans can be borrowed or hired if required.

- **Commode** This piece of 'furniture' is necessary in the later stages of an illness but can also be useful if your relative needs to use the toilet during the night.

- **Sliding sheets** Made of a slippery nylon fabric, the two surfaces slide easily when placed together to move a person in any direction on chairs, beds and car seats.

- **Moving aids (hand held)** These firm, flat, plastic supports can be placed under the thighs or the back of an individual and held by two people to make lifting in a chair or bed easier. Alternatively, a curved banana-shaped board can be placed between a chair and the bed (or wheelchair) to slide the individual across so that they do not have to be raised into a standing position. Using aids such as these puts less strain on frail limbs and shoulder joints – for both the individual and their carers.

- **Mechanical hoists** These operate by electricity or hydraulic power and are used mainly in a care home setting by professional carers for people who are very difficult to move; hoists can also be recommended for use at home, after assessment.

- **Bed and chair raisers** These look like heavy-duty plastic flower-pots and are excellent for raising furniture by several inches to ease the strain of bending and moving.

- **Sheepskins and special mattresses** Several types are available to help protect vulnerable pressure points when a person becomes chair- or bed-ridden.

- **Pillow support or back rest** Several types are available.

- **Handrails and ramps** These can be positioned at various places, such as the bathroom and at the entrances to the house.

- **Bath aids** These range from basic non-slip mats to mechanical lifts.

- **Adapted cutlery and crockery** For general eating and drinking, or for kitchen use if your relative enjoys helping with the cooking or wants to make a hot drink.

■ **Two-way 'baby listening' system, portable/mobile telephone, answering machine or entryphone** All of these offer a means of communication without the need to rush.

Laura

'The commode was brilliant. It had wheels and we could push it right over the toilet seat, so there was no need to waste energy struggling to move in a small space.'

Equipment can be hired or borrowed from several organisations; the main providers are social services, NHS trusts and voluntary organisations. Your first point of call for information and assessment is an occupational therapist (OT). They work towards restoring and maintaining levels of independence and reducing the impact of illness. Occupational therapists may be based with social services or the NHS, depending on whether your relative has been referred to them because of a health or a social need. Ask your doctor to make a referral for a home visit if you are unsure which agency to approach. Equipment supplied by the NHS is lent free of charge. Unfortunately, the waiting lists are long in many areas.

Grants may be available through your relative's local authority if they need help with major adaptations to the home, such as a stairlift or adapting a bathroom. An assessment for this is made by an occupational therapist.

For more information

ⓘ **The Disabled Living Foundation** offers advice on aids and equipment (address on page 182).

ⓘ **The Disability Living Centres Council** (address on page 182) can tell you about the centre nearest you, where you can see and try out aids and equipment.

ⓘ The local branches of the **British Red Cross** or **St John Ambulance** give advice and arrange the hire or loan of equipment. Look in the telephone directory for a contact number, or ask the community nurse for a referral.

ⓘ Age Concern Factsheet 42 *Disability Equipment and How to Get It* (see page 197 for details of how to obtain factsheets).

Terminal care

Gill

'Somehow I felt less upset when my husband died at home because we were in our own house. I know that not everyone can manage care at home, but I had lots of help from the community nurses and my family.'

Reg

'My wife was moved to a hospital just before she died. I couldn't care for her as well as the nurses because she needed constant attention. She was looked after so well I felt I had made the right decision.'

Caring for a relative with a terminal illness at home is a time of great emotional and physical strain. It is not easy to make predictions about how long the final stages of an illness will last or how much care an individual person may need. People whose health is deteriorating have good and bad days and may remain on a plateau for quite a while, supported by medication and nursing care, before they finally slip into unconsciousness.

If you are continuing to nurse your relative at home in the final stages of their illness, you will be offered support from the local community nursing team. They assess how much care is needed and will visit several times a day to wash and turn your relative. In some areas there are special flexible services that provide help to settle patients down at night and give painkilling and sedative drugs, and all-night nursing services to sit with very ill people. Your relative's doctor will make the necessary arrangements or you can contact a community nurse direct if the service is available for your use.

You may be concerned about what to do and how you will cope. Try to bring yourself to talk to a nurse about this and let them advise you about what steps you need to take. Being with a loved one who dies at home can be a very tranquil experience, knowing that you have helped them die peacefully in their own surroundings. If your relative needs to be admitted to hospital or a hospice for their last days, the staff will do everything possible to make them and your family feel comfortable. Ask the staff to let you help with the care, so that you can remain involved and continue to do your best for your relative.

Dying with dignity

There are many ways in which family, friends and medical staff can help to ensure that the *expected* death of a person is approached with dignity. It is probable that in the terminal stages of any illness the person (if they are conscious) will be aware of their deterioration and the changes that are taking place in their body. Some people recognise the inevitability of death and become peaceful, whilst others continue to struggle and are less accepting. Sometimes the ill person and family members are at different stages of acceptance; in this case it may help to talk to each other or to someone who is less involved. If the ill person has accepted that death is close, relatives must respect this feeling and not beg them to hang on to life. We have certain obligations towards a dying person. In practical terms, these focus on their right to be kept clean, warm, comfortable and free of pain. Perhaps less easy to understand is any need for emotional and spiritual fulfilment, often because a person close to death is unable to express in words what they actually feel or desire. Sitting quietly by the bedside may be sufficient.

Melly, a community nurse

'Being close by is very important. If you are able, talk to your relative, ask them about their wishes and give them an opportunity to talk and feel at peace. Even if your relative is unable to respond, they may still be able to hear you. Be careful about discussing insensitive matters within their hearing.'

Over the final days, if appropriate, your relative may wish to spend time doing some of the following things:

- Talking with the people they hold dear, including friends – to reminisce about past times; tell them about their love, which may include saying sorry for past disagreements; and to be reassured that someone will talk to younger children.

- Talking about their fears of death and what might lie ahead, perhaps with a non-family member so that privacy is maintained.

- Seeking reassurance that they are not being a nuisance, particularly if they lose control of bodily functions.

- Knowing that all their affairs have been put in order, including the wish to make or amend a will, and to feel that they will have left sufficient means for a spouse or other dependant to live in reasonable comfort.

- Having someone sitting with them at the time of death and to receive any spiritual or religious rites as part of their cultural belief.

- Helping plan their own funeral service by choosing hymns, psalms and readings.

- Knowing that a final resting place for their body or ashes has been agreed and that any requests to be buried or cremated in special clothes or wearing a piece of jewellery will be respected.

Helen, a nurse

'Even though I have worked in a hospital for years, it is not easy to comfort a dying person as our society has few words to use in a situation about which we have no direct experience. I suggest that relatives listen with sympathy and offer words of gentle support so that the dying person can talk about their fears.'

Most people hold some fears about dying, especially when they can sense that life is drawing to a close. They may experience deep anxiety and even panic at the uncertainty ahead. Apprehension about dying is a natural fear that should never be suppressed or dismissed as foolish by healthy people. Until faced with the reality of death, few people ever think about its implications for themselves or how they will react. People's fears tend to focus on similar issues. For example:

■ the process of dying and what happens following death;
■ possible forthcoming judgement, depending on their religious beliefs;
■ losing control, especially increasing dependence on others and incontinence;
■ dying alone or in an unpleasant manner; or
■ being buried or cremated alive.

Recognising that death is imminent

Timing matters greatly and many people find it easier to cope with the thought of the forthcoming period if they have some idea when to expect the death.

Helen, a nurse

'Many relatives ask professional carers "how long will he/she live?". Clearly, there can be no definite and precise answer to this question but it may be possible for nurses to be given some idea of timescale. For example, if someone is already unconscious, the final time is unlikely to be drawn out. This period may last days but could more easily be expressed in hours. We try to give a gentle warning at this stage to help prepare you for the approaching death and support you to accept the certainty of the situation.'

At the time of death you may wish to sit by the bedside and hold your relative. When a person is dying their breathing often sounds noisy and their body may become restless. These changes are part of the process of dying; they are not signs of distress. A dying person usually slips into a coma and is not aware of these actions. Breathing gradually slows down and stops. If you wish to check that death has occurred, you can also feel for a pulse at the wrist. Make a note of the time of death. Afterwards it is all right to sit quietly with your relative for a while and adjust your thoughts.

After a while you must inform someone of the death. If you are in a hospital the staff will be close by and a nurse may be with you at the time of death. If you are at home you, or another family member, must telephone your relative's doctor so that he/she can confirm the death before issuing the Medical Certificate of Cause of Death. The GP or a member of the hospital staff will explain what to do next. (See pages 129–131 for information about how to register a death.)

Laying out your relative

You may like to wash your relative and perhaps dress them in clean clothes or help a nurse to do this. The hospital staff or undertaker will do this job if you would prefer not to and you can stay with the body, or not, as you choose. If your relative has died at home, you can call the undertaker at any time of the day or night.

Helen, a nurse

'People behave in different ways immediately after the death of a loved person. How you actually feel and behave may be different to how you imagine you will respond; there are no right or wrong feelings at this time.'

Feelings of bereavement following a death

For any person, the term 'bereavement' means more than the loss of a loved one. It encompasses the loss of a wide range of life experiences and 'situations' they hold dear, such as their relationship with the person (eg parent/child), a useful or satisfying role (eg gardener or housekeeper), the sale of a well-loved family home, etc.

Bereaved people describe similar feelings and often experience phases of grief that have been identified as common to most people. The way in which people show their grief is a personal matter, so it is wrong to lump everyone into a category whereby all bereaved people behave alike. However, it does appear that many people follow a comparable path, so at some point you are likely to feel:

- shock, numbness, pain, disbelief;
- fear, guilt, anger, resentment;
- signs of withdrawal, apathy, quietness, lack of interest;
- ideas of bargaining, searching, questioning, yearning, wanting to 'put the clock back';
- signs and symptoms of depression, emptiness, deep anxiety, overwhelming sense of loss, over-dependence; and
- signs of acceptance, recognition, relief, moving forward to recovery.

While you and your family are going through the early stages of bereavement, do not expect to move forward very quickly. Anticipate, accept and even encourage outward signs of emotion. Take each day at a time: it is not uncommon to move forwards and backwards along a continuum of grief. Gently introduce the view that meaningful life did not necessarily finish on the day your loved one died. Pose the question 'what would they have wanted me to do'? Suggest to yourself that your loved one might want you to get better, and gradually let go of the past. Be clear that moving forward is not about forgetting the earlier life together, or about being disloyal to a memory. Rather, it is about cherishing old times in a realistic way.

If you find that your grief is not abating, it may help to seek advice from a specialist bereavement counsellor, such as CRUSE – Bereavement Care, which offers information, support and encouragement to bereaved people and their families (see address on page 182).

For more information

ⓘ *Caring for someone who is dying*, published by Age Concern Books (see page 192).

Conclusion

The decision whether to look after your relative at home or arrange care in a care home will be based on a number of factors – the wishes of the person concerned; your ability to give quality care; the support that other family members can give; and the type and amount of care that is needed. It's not an easy decision and cannot be taken lightly. Caring for someone is a time-consuming and strenuous job that draws heavily on the personal resources of the main carer. This task is almost impossible to undertake single-handed and relies on the support of the professional services as well as family and friends. If the care is long term, it can put a strain on marriages and stretch finances.

Whatever your initial decision may be, it is important that you review it from time to time and accept that no carer can ever make a promise that is binding forever.

The next chapter will help you to deal with the affairs of the person you care for.

5 Dealing with everyday affairs

One of the main roles of a carer is that of helping to manage the financial and legal affairs of their relative. This may be because they have become too physically disabled or mentally confused to manage alone, or because they feel unsure about dealing with people in 'authority' and feel reluctant to take decisions alone about complex issues. You might have to take over responsibility gradually or swiftly, depending on the state of health and wishes of your relative.

This chapter outlines the services and agencies you could turn to for help and describes some of the welfare benefits and legal procedures that you and your relative may wish to investigate. It is unlikely that you will require all of the information at any one time, so return to the relevant sections as necessary during your relative's illness. One section, however, that you may wish to find out more about, is that relating to 'living wills' – a form of advance directive which enables people to set up a written document stating their wishes about how they would want to be treated at the time of their death.

Dealing with the affairs of another person is a serious business and you may feel daunted at first. However, there are people who will help and advise you and there are many safeguards in place to protect you and your relative. It would be wise to cover yourself by seeking advice from a reputable source – a solicitor, an accountant, a bank or a voluntary organisation – before you enter into legal contracts or make any major decisions, especially concerning property or the management of your relative's money.

Sylvia

'After my husband had a heart attack I took over the financial planning. I soon got the hang of bank statements and the bank helped me set up monthly payments for all our main bills.'

Finding out about help and advice

Getting the right information needs mental stamina, creative thinking and a mind that can jump like a grasshopper – or so it feels on occasions, particularly if you are tied to the house. Look out for sound, informative articles published by the local and national press and programmes broadcast on radio and television. The material is often well researched, unbiased and aimed at the general public. Investigate the huge range of information available on the various websites. If you do not have access to the Internet yourself, it's one area where a younger family member or friend would no doubt be keen to demonstrate their knowledge and skills. Alternatively, the majority of public libraries provide Internet points and someone would help you go 'online'.

For more detailed information, advice and advocacy there are many organisations that offer carers a service at local and national level; some are specialists in their field and others provide general information and act as signposts to the specialists. Most organisations offer facilities for disabled people and some information in minority languages. The main agencies to contact are listed in the table on the next four pages.

Elsie

'Tom had always done the paperwork at home, so when he wasn't up to it I asked for some financial advice at the Citizens Advice Bureau. They helped me fill out our tax form.'

Organisation	Services offered	How to contact
Advocacy services	An advocacy service (advocate) will represent and speak on behalf of people who are not skilled or confident to do so themselves, to help them to obtain and make best use of local services	Local telephone directory or ask at local Citizens Advice Bureau or Age Concern
Age Concern	Provides information practical help, social activities and a range of publications for older people and carers	Local telephone directory or address on page 191. Information Line: 0800 00 99 66
Benefit Enquiry Line for people with disabilities	Provides advice and information about disability benefits. Staff can arrange for help with completing forms over the phone for benefits such as Attendance Allowance and Disability Living Allowance	Freephone: 0800 88 22 00 Textphone: 0800 24 33 55
Citizens Advice Bureaux	Free, confidential advice and information on a wide range of legal, financial,	Local telephone directory or in *Yellow Pages*

	social and consumer problems, and help with form filling and representation at hearings	under 'Counselling and advice'
Consumer services departments	Offer information to local people about the services and facilities available from their own organisation. They are usually provided by all statutory agencies (eg local councils, health trusts and social services departments) and many services industries (eg water, gas and electricity)	Local telephone directory under appropriate agency
Council for Voluntary Service (CVS)	Information about the voluntary sector locally	Local telephone directory; national address on page 186
Counsel and Care	Charity providing information, advice and practical help to older people and carers, particularly advice about care at home or in a care home	Address on page 181
Disablement Information and Advice Lines (DIAL)	Advice on aids and equipment and disability services	Local telephone directory; national address on page 183
Disability Living Centres	Have aids and equipment you can see and try out	National address on page 182
Disabled Living Foundation	Information on aids and equipment	Address on page 182

Housing advice	Many local authorities provide a housing advice service to local residents in owner-occupied or rented accommodation	Local telephone directory
Independent advice centres	Independent organisations in most urban areas and some rural areas, offering free advice on problems relating to benefits, debt and work issues	Advice UK (page 177) or local telephone directory
Independent Complaints Advocacy Services	Help people who want to complain about health services	NHS Direct or the local PALS (see below)
Neighbourhood schemes	Many local authorities and voluntary groups run community schemes offering a range of information and support to local people	Local telephone directory under name of council; or ask at local library or Council for Voluntary Service
NHS Direct	Provides confidential health advice and information, 24 hours a day, seven days a week. Helplines are staffed by qualified nurses and health information advisors	Tel: 0845 46 47
PALS (Patient Advice and Liaison Services)	If you want advice, or to complain, about your relative's treatment, there is a PALS in every NHS Trust	Ask at the surgery or hospital, or contact NHS Direct

111

Pension Service	Provides information about State Pensions and other pension-related entitlements	Tel: 0845 606 0625; (www.thepensionservice.gov.uk) or local telephone directory
Public library	Excellent sources of local information, books, videos, directories, quality journals, many daily newspapers and local addresses	Personal visit, telephone, or limited home delivery

State benefits

The benefits system is complex and can only be covered broadly here because each person has individual needs, and the information, amounts given and eligibility are subject to change. The Department for Work and Pensions (DWP; formerly the Department of Social Security) is the government department responsible for benefits. The benefits listed below are those mostly applicable to an older age group. The full range of benefits is listed in leaflets available from the DWP, most local authorities, the Citizens Advice Bureaux and some post offices. A useful one to look out for is leaflet SD4 *Caring for Someone*, which describes benefits for carers and disabled people.

Maria, a benefits adviser

'Many older people and carers say that they feel trapped and at the end of their tether. They think that they can manage and continue to struggle when they might be entitled to make a claim.'

There are millions of pounds of unclaimed benefits, particularly those targeted at older people. If your relative is reluctant to claim benefits, try to persuade them that they are not asking for charity: they or their spouse have probably contributed far more over the years than they will claim back. Many carers claim on behalf of a relative without realising that they might be eligible for benefits in their own right.

Jeff, a benefits adviser

'Ask about benefits or you won't know what is available. It's really worth getting a knowledgeable person to check out your circumstances. Ask for help at the Citizens Advice Bureau.'

Ahmed, a benefits adviser

'People who help with benefits are aware that completing claim forms is a complicated business and that you might be put off because you feel too tired or distressed to bother. An adviser at the Citizens Advice Bureau or the Jobcentre Plus office would help you make a claim.'

For telephone advice about claims and information, contact the Benefit Enquiry Line for people with a disability on Freephone 0800 88 22 00. If you need information about benefits in other languages, contact your local Jobcentre Plus office (listed in your local telephone directory), or The Pension Service on 0845 606 0625 and you will be connected with the pension centre covering your area.

People claiming a State benefit must meet strict criteria; some benefits are means-tested or taxed or both. The introduction of new tax credits in April 2003 has meant that certain tax credits might be available to people aged 60 years and above, as well as eligible families. Make your claim as soon as possible as some benefits cannot be backdated. If you or your relative disagrees with a decision made by the DWP, you have the right to ask for your case to be looked at again and/or appeal against a decision. There are strict deadlines for lodging an appeal, so if

113

you are concerned you should seek advice urgently. Many claims which were unsuccessful at first are granted on appeal.

Benefits for the person you look after

Attendance Allowance

Attendance Allowance is for people aged 65 years or over (whether or not they live alone) who need help with personal care, supervision or someone to watch over them due to an illness or disability. It is tax-free and not means-tested and not dependent on National Insurance contributions, but to qualify the person must normally have needed help with personal care for a period of six months. People who are terminally ill can qualify immediately. There are two rates (higher and lower), according to how much care is needed and whether the care is needed during the day or at night, or both. Get a claim pack (AA1 or DLA1 for Disability Living Allowance: see below) by phoning the Benefit Enquiry Line on 0800 88 22 00, sending off the slip from leaflet DS702 (DS704 for DLA), or from some local advice agencies.

Disability Living Allowance (DLA)

Disability Living Allowance is for people who make a claim before the age of 65 years and who have care and/or mobility needs. To qualify people normally must have satisfied the conditions for at least three months and be expected to continue to do so for at least a further six months. It has a care component for people who need help with personal care, supervision or someone to watch over them, and a mobility component for people who need help with getting around. DLA is tax-free and not means-tested and not dependent on National Insurance contributions. The person receiving the allowance is free to spend the money however they choose; it does not have to be spent on care. The mobility component has two rates and the care component three; these are awarded according to the needs of the disabled person. People who are terminally ill can qualify for DLA without the three-month period. DLA is a gateway to other types of help (eg the Blue Badge scheme, which gives holders special parking privileges).

Statutory Sick Pay (SSP)

SSP is paid by the employer instead of wages for up to 28 weeks to someone who is too sick or disabled to work.

Incapacity Benefit (IB)

Incapacity Benefit is for people under State Pension age who are unable to work because of an illness or disability and who have paid enough National Insurance contributions. The benefit is given at different rates, depending on how long the person has been unable to work. For the first 28 weeks a claimant is assessed on their ability to carry out their own job, based normally on information given on medical certificates provided by the GP. After 28 weeks the person is assessed on how well they can carry out a range of work-related activities, called the 'personal capability assessment'. This assessment is carried out through completion of a questionnaire by the claimant and possibly also an examination by an appointed doctor. Some people may qualify for extra money if their husband or wife is over 60 years or they have dependent children.

Benefits for carers

Carer's Allowance

To qualify for Carer's Allowance (which was previously called Invalid Care Allowance) you must be providing care for at least 35 hours per week to a person who is receiving Attendance Allowance or Constant Attendance Allowance or the middle or highest rates of the care component of Disability Living Allowance. The person you are caring for does not have to be a relative and may live separately or with you. There is now no upper age limit for claiming Carer's Allowance, although if you are receiving a State Pension or another benefit you may not receive the allowance on top of this. You can have a job and still get Carer's Allowance but you must not earn above a certain amount (after deduction of allowable expenses). The allowance is taxable. Carer's Allowance can be backdated for three months. Ask for claim pack

DS700 from your local social security office or from the Benefit Enquiry Line on Freephone 0800 88 22 00 or on the Internet from the DWP website (www.dwp.gov.uk) where you can also claim online.

The carer premium/addition

This is an extra amount of money paid to a carer as part of their Income Support, Pension Credit, Housing Benefit or Council Tax Benefit. You will be entitled to the carer premium if you are entitled to Carer's Allowance (even if you don't get Carer's Allowance because you are already getting a State Pension or other benefits).

Home Responsibilities Protection (HRP)

Home Responsibilities Protection is not a true benefit but a scheme which helps protect your Basic State Pension. If you are unable to pay National Insurance contributions or have not paid enough for any year of caring, you can claim HRP, which helps towards qualifying for State Pension. If you receive Carer's Allowance, you are normally entitled to National Insurance credits (free contributions on your NI record) and will not usually need HRP. If you get Income Support because you are caring for someone, you will usually get HRP automatically. If you cannot claim Carer's Allowance for any reason but still care for over 35 hours per week for someone who receives Attendance Allowance, Constant Attendance Allowance or the high or middle rate of the care component of Disability Living Allowance, you may be able to get Home Responsibilities Protection. Ask for claim form CF411 from the local Jobcentre Plus office.

Benefits for people on a low income

Pension Credit

Pension Credit is a social security entitlement for people aged 60 and over with low and modest incomes, and was introduced in October 2003. You do not need to have paid National Insurance contributions to qualify for Pension Credit, but your income and any savings and capital over a certain level will be taken into account. It is not taxable.

It has two parts – the guarantee credit and the savings credit. The guarantee credit has replaced Income Support for people aged 60 and over. It tops up income to a designated level. Unlike Income Support, there is no upper savings level. The savings credit is intended to reward people aged 65 and over for a proportion of the savings and income they have for their retirement. People may be entitled to the guarantee credit or the savings credit or both.

For a couple, one of you applies on behalf of both partners (a partner means a spouse or two people who live together as if married to each other). The person who applies must be at least 60 years of age; it does not matter if their partner is under 60. To qualify for the savings credit at least one of you must be 65 or over.

To qualify for Pension Credit, the person is subject to an assessment of weekly net income (after deductions) and savings. Only certain types of income are counted, including pensions, most State benefits (eg Carer's Allowance) and earnings from a job. Some benefits, such as Attendance Allowance and Disability Living Allowance, are not taken into account. The amount of savings a person has is taken into account above £6,000 in 2004 (£10,000 for people living permanently in a care home). There are higher rates of Pension Credit for certain groups of people (those who are severely disabled, carers of severely disabled people and those who have certain housing costs).

There is a special Pension Credit claim line on 0800 99 1234, but if you prefer you can contact a local advice agency or the local Pension Service.

Income Support

Income Support is a means-tested benefit paid to someone aged under 60 whose income and savings are below a certain level. It is paid to people who do not have to sign on for work; for example people who can't work because they are carers or people who are sick or disabled. Income Support can be paid to top up other benefits or earnings from part-time work (including self-employment), provided the person works

117

for fewer than 16 hours per week. To claim, contact your local Jobcentre Plus office.

Housing Benefit

Housing Benefit helps with the cost of rent for people on a low income. It is generally only awarded to people who have no more than £16,000 in savings, although the savings limit will not apply to some people receiving Pension Credit.

Council Tax Benefit

This benefit helps with the Council Tax (called rates in Northern Ireland) for people on a low income. As with Housing Benefit, it is generally only awarded to people who have no more than £16,000 in savings, although the savings limit will not apply to some people receiving Pension Credit.

Social Fund

The Social Fund provides grants and loans to help people with expenses that are difficult to pay for out of regular income. Budgeting Loans, Crisis Loans and Community Care Grants are discretionary, but the other payments described below are made to everyone who satisfies the conditions.

Budgeting Loans may be available to people receiving Pension Credit or certain other benefits (for at least 26 weeks) to help spread the cost of important expenses. Interest-free loans (which have to be paid back) may be available for a range of specific items – for example to buy furniture, clothing or pay travel expenses.

Crisis Loans are for people with no savings or access to funds to help them cope with an emergency or disaster, such as fire or burglary, that puts the family at serious health or safety risk. Applicants do not have to be in receipt of other State benefits. The interest-free loan has to be paid back.

Community Care Grants are available to people on Pension Credit and certain other State benefits and to people who will be discharged from care within six weeks and are likely to receive these benefits on discharge. The grants do not have to be repaid, but the amount of any savings over £1,000 (£500 for people under 60) will be deducted from the grant. The grants are available for purposes such as help with moving out of care or to enable someone to remain living at home.

Cold Weather Payments are paid automatically to recipients of Pension Credit, when the actual or forecast average temperature goes down to freezing (zero degrees Celsius) or below for seven consecutive days.

Winter Fuel Payments provide help with the cost of fuel bills for pensioner households. A one-off annual payment is normally paid automatically to most people aged 60 years and over, although some need to make an application. There are no income or savings limits. An extra amount is paid where someone in the household is aged 80 or over. To claim, contact the Pension Service's Winter Fuel Payment Helpline on 08459 15 15 15.

Funeral Payments may be available to some people receiving means-tested benefits, who are responsible for the funeral of a partner, close relative or close friend. The payment may have to be repaid from any money or property left by the person who died. Any savings might affect how much the applicant gets, and the DWP must agree that it is reasonable for the person to be responsible for the funeral before they will agree any payment.

Bereavement benefits

People widowed below State Pension age may be entitled to bereavement benefits such as the Bereavement Payment or Bereavement Allowance. For more information, see social security guide NP45 *A Guide to Bereavement Benefits*.

For more information

ⓘ *Your Rights: A Guide to Money Benefits for Older People*, published annually by Age Concern Books (see page 196).

ⓘ Age Concern Factsheets (see page 197 for details of how to obtain factsheets):
17 *Housing Benefit and Council Tax Benefit*
18 *A Brief Guide to Money Benefits*
34 *Attendance Allowance and Disability Living Allowance*
48 *Pension Credit*
49 *Help from the Social Fund*

NHS benefits

Most of the treatment given under the NHS is free, but there are some things for which most people have to pay part or all of the cost. Help with health costs is available for people who receive certain State benefits or are on a low income. These might help your relative with charges for prescriptions and eye tests (although these are free if they are 60 or over), glasses, dentures and dental treatment, wigs and bandages, and with fares to hospital to receive NHS treatment. Some people (eg those receiving Pension Credit guarantee) are automatically exempted from some of these charges. Other people on a low income may get help if they apply on form HC1. Ask for details at your surgery, hospital clinic or a pharmacy.

For more information

ⓘ Department of Health leaflet HC11 *Help with Health Costs.*

ⓘ Age Concern Information Sheet IS20 *Help with Health Costs for Older People.*

Taxation

Inland Revenue

Home visits can be arranged for enquiries about personal income and other taxes if your relative is unable to get to a local office. A range of information is available in booklets, many of which appear in minority languages, Braille and large print, and in audio cassettes.

For more information

ⓘ Age Concern Factsheet 15 *Income Tax and Older People* (see page 197 for details of how to obtain factsheets).

ⓘ *Your Taxes and Savings: A Guide for Older People*, published annually by Age Concern Books (see page 196).

Council Tax

Council Tax, collected by local councils as a contribution towards local services, is assessed according to the value of each property and the number of adults in it. There are reductions, discounts and exemptions available that may help you as a carer and your relative. These relate to empty dwellings (you may have left your home to go and care for your relative or they may have moved in with you), to homes with substantial adaptations that are placed in a lower valuation band, and to people whose presence in a household is disregarded, thus leading to a lower bill. Once your Council Tax liability is assessed, you or your relative may be able to claim Council Tax Benefit (see above) to help pay. Get help from an advice agency or your local authority.

For more information

ⓘ Age Concern Factsheet 21 *The Council Tax and Older People* (see page 197 for details of how to obtain factsheets).

Grants from private organisations

If your relative has checked that they are getting all the benefits that they are entitled to and they are still finding it hard to manage financially, they could try asking for help from charities or benevolent funds. Many local and national trusts and charities have grants to help you purchase one-off items of equipment or pay for respite care. The qualifying criteria vary; for example, a benevolent fund may be open only to certain categories of people living in a defined area or connected to a particular occupation.

For more information

ⓘ **Ask a local advice agency**, such as the Citizens Advice Bureau.

ⓘ Two national organisations, **The Association of Charity Officers** (address on page 177) and **Charity Search** (address on page 180), can help put people in contact with charities and benevolent funds.

Managing somebody's financial affairs

There are several ways that you can take over responsibility for your relative's financial affairs, depending on the state of their physical and mental health. Be aware that their needs may alter rapidly, and be ready to take any necessary steps to increase your level of responsibility before it becomes too late to make changes.

Agent

If the person you care for is mentally capable, but unable to get out, they can still retain overall responsibility for their money but appoint you as their 'agent'. You would be able to collect their pension or benefits on their behalf, but not spend it. An agency card can be obtained from the social security office stating that you, as the named person, are authorised to collect the money.

The Government is phasing in changes to the way that benefits and pensions are paid so that by 2005 most people will receive their money paid directly into a bank, building society or post office account. If you collect money on behalf of your relative, you will need to check how you can do this with the different types of accounts. If you are not sure which of the options are suitable, get further advice from the issuing post office or a local advice agency.

Appointee

If your relative is not able to manage their money, you may be able to become their 'appointee' (you have to be in regular contact with them in order to qualify). As an appointee, you will be responsible for withdrawing money for any benefits your relative receives, on their behalf, but you will also have other responsibilities. It may be best to get some advice before taking on this responsibility as there are administrative tasks involved.

Powers of attorney

Power of attorney is a legal document which gives someone the legal right to manage another person's affairs, for example if they are ill in hospital or away on holiday. The **ordinary power of attorney** can be set up for cases where the person is able to give sound instructions (it can be reviewed if the person recovers and wishes to resume control of their affairs); however, it will become invalid if the person becomes mentally incapable. To avoid this problem, most solicitors suggest an **Enduring Power of Attorney** which, after registration, remains valid if your relative becomes too confused to manage their own affairs, provided it is registered with the Public Guardianship Office. It is important that you both take independent advice before setting this up, as it carries a heavy responsibility for the carer that could involve selling property and dealing with taxation. The procedure is very formal so, although not essential, it's usual to set it up through a solicitor, although you can buy a document from a legal stationer.

Court of Protection

The Court of Protection is the body charged with a duty to provide financial protection services for people who are not able to manage their own financial affairs because of mental incapacity. If your relative becomes mentally incapable of looking after their own affairs before they have given you an Enduring Power of Attorney, you may apply for help from the Court of Protection. In England and Wales the Court of Protection can appoint a 'receiver' and in Northern Ireland the Office of Care and Protection can appoint a 'controller' (usually a relative, friend or solicitor), who can have authority to do anything that the person would do if they were still capable of acting for their own benefit. Different rules apply in Scotland (see below). Expenses incurred will come out of your relative's funds.

Applying to the Court of Protection is costly and complicated, so it is better to avoid it if you can by encouraging your relative to create an EPA in good time.

If you do not wish to undertake this duty, a bank or solicitor will act as receiver in your place, for a fee. Contact the Customer Services Unit of the Public Guardianship Office (address on page 187).

For more information

ⓘ Social security leaflet GL21 *A Helping Hand for Benefits? How Somebody with an Illness or Disability Can Get Help to Collect or Deal with Social Security Benefits*.

ⓘ Age Concern Factsheet 22 *Legal Arrangements for Managing Financial Affairs* (see page 197 for details of how to obtain factsheets).

ⓘ **The Public Guardianship Office** (address on page 187) produces a number of free explanatory booklets and leaflets.

Managing financial affairs in Scotland

The Adults with Incapacity (Scotland) Act 2000 changed the law relating to the management of financial affairs. Individuals can arrange for their welfare to be safeguarded and their affairs to be properly managed in the future, should their capacity deteriorate. They do this by giving another person the **Continuing Power of Attorney** to look after their affairs.

All continuing and welfare Powers of Attorney granted after April 2001 have to be registered with the Office of the Public Guardian to be effective. Individuals can also apply to the Public Guardian to access the funds of an adult incapable of managing these funds. Since April 2002, authorised care establishments can manage a limited amount of funds and property of residents who are unable to do this for themselves.

For more information

i Age Concern Factsheet 22s *Legal Arrangements for Managing Financial Affairs* (the Scottish version).

i **The Office of the Public Guardian** (see address on page 187) can provide information about Continuing Power of Attorney and financial or welfare guardianship.

Making a Will

Your relative may talk to you about making a Will, or they may wish to add to or alter an existing Will, if it was made a long time ago and their situation has changed. When someone is ill, they begin to think more about their personal affairs and may ask you to help them sort out the legal arrangements. If you feel uncomfortable or unsure about doing this task, ask someone else to help – perhaps a friend who is sensible and practical but less personally involved. If your relative is unable to go out, many solicitors offer a home service to help people write a Will. Look in the *Yellow Pages* or ask at the Citizens Advice Bureau for details.

Some people draw up their own Wills. This is quite in order as long as the correct procedures are followed. The Will must be written clearly, and signed and dated in the presence of two (or just one in Scotland) independent witnesses (or relatives who are not beneficiaries or their spouses). The Will must name one or more people who are willing to act as executors (ie the ones responsible for seeing that the instructions written in the Will are properly carried out). Executors can be relatives, friends or professional people who provide this service as part of their job (eg an accountant or a solicitor). A person who acts as an executor can also be named in the Will as a beneficiary. Information packs and Will forms are available from many stationers, and details of other booklets are given below. (If you live in Scotland, make sure that the information in the pack you buy does cover the law in Scotland.)

If your relative's affairs are not simple or straightforward, it would be wise to ask a solicitor to draw up the Will; their fees for home and office appointments vary, so telephone and ask for a quotation before booking a home visit.

Why is a Will important?

Some people wrongly assume that if their affairs are straightforward they do not need to make a Will, because all of their belongings will go directly to their closest relative. But there are strict laws about how a person's estate (the name given to their money and property) is divided up, and it can be complicated and costly to sort out the affairs of someone who has died without making a Will (intestate).

The following 'down to earth' comments from a solicitor should help if your relative is undecided and asks your opinion about the benefits of making a Will:

■ You don't have to have a lot of money to make a Will. Making a Will is about making sure that your possessions go to the person(s) you want to receive them.

■ You mustn't feel morbid about making a Will; all you are doing is setting out your plan as to how your assets are to be split up when you die.

■ If you do not make a Will, the rules governing intestacy apply, which may mean that your assets will be given to relatives you do not know or even want to know.

■ Just saying to someone that a treasured ornament or a piece of jewellery is theirs when you die is not good enough. The only safe way of making sure that happens is to put it in a Will.

Living wills

Eric, a general practitioner

'I always take account of a good advance directive when caring for a patient who is in a potentially terminal phase. Doctors believe that they are a help rather than a hindrance.'

Do not be afraid to talk with your relative openly about their wishes in matters surrounding their death as it is very probable that they would want to share their feelings with someone close to them. Many people feel the need to attend to their affairs sensibly whilst they are capable of thinking coherently. A phrase often used to describe this period is 'putting your house in order'. An 'advance directive' is a form of 'living will' and is an example of this type of forward planning which covers, specifically, a person's desire to exercise some control over the manner in which they die – within legal boundaries. However, with the taboos that still persist about death, many people do not always find it easy to broach the topic. Inevitably, some people never have the opportunity to make their wishes known, leading to the situation where they die in circumstances that are less than ideal for them.

In recent years living wills have been actively promoted by some organisations and professional people, as a means of giving individuals some pre-considered choice about such issues as medical treatment. At the time of writing there is no primary legislation covering advance directives in England, Wales and Northern Ireland, and there is no guarantee that people who have made such a statement will achieve their wishes. However, a number of court decisions and government statements have established that a living will can be legally effective for refusal of treatment if it is properly drafted and if it applies to the situation which arises. The Adults with Incapacity (Scotland) Act 2000 allows for a proxy decision-maker (a 'welfare attorney') legally to refuse treatment on behalf of an incapacitated adult.

127

It is not necessary to use a lawyer to prepare an advance directive. However, the ethical, legal and practical issues are complex, so do not attempt to draw up a document without first researching the topic thoroughly and taking some form of professional advice. For example, the Age Concern England book on the topic (see below) and the Citizens Advice Bureau would be good starting points. The Fact Box below gives a brief example of the subject areas a family would need to understand:

Fact Box

A valid advance directive requires:

- evidence that the person was competent at the time of writing it;
- evidence that the person is fully informed about the nature of their directive and its implications;
- evidence that the person has made the decision outlined in the advance directive without pressure or coercion; and
- evidence that the directive has not been changed.

(Source: *Their Rights: Advance Directives and Living Wills Explored,* Age Concern Books.)

It would be very important to discuss the situation with your relative's doctor at an early stage of the process. Their GP knows their health history well and can help families understand the treatment choices that might need to be faced. It is also vital that all health professionals know about the statement and can understand the wishes it contains.

For more information

ⓘ *Their Rights: Advance Directives and Living Wills Explored,* published by Age Concern Books (see page 195).

Registering a death

A death must be registered (usually in the district where the death occurred) within five days (eight days in Scotland), unless the registrar says this period can be extended. The person registering the death can make a formal declaration giving the details required in any other registration district in England and Wales. This will then be passed to the registrar for the district where the death occurred, who will issue the death certificate and any other documentation. (In Scotland, it can be registered in the office for the area where the deceased person normally lived.)

Some offices operate an appointment system, so telephone as soon as you receive the medical certificate of cause of death. Whether the death occurs in a hospital or at home, you will be given the same type of certificate. The address and telephone number of the local office are in the telephone directory under 'Registration of births, deaths and marriages'; leaflets are available from the office.

In some circumstances the death will be referred to the coroner; if this is the case, you will be advised what to do. A coroner is usually involved when the death is sudden, unnatural, unexplained, or attended by suspicious circumstances. A common reason is because the GP has not seen the person during the 14 days before their death.

It is usual for a relative to register the death but this can be done by another person. Allow a reasonable amount of time to complete the formalities, although it will help if you can have certain pieces of information to hand. The Registrar will want to know the following information about the deceased person:

- the date and place of death;
- your relative's full name (and maiden name if appropriate);
- their date and place of birth;
- their occupation (and that of the husband for a married woman or widow);
- their usual address;

129

- whether they were in receipt of a State Pension or other benefits;
- the date of birth of the surviving spouse if appropriate; and
- their NHS number or actual medical card, and birth and marriage certificates, if available.

The registrar should give you:

- **A certificate for burial or cremation** (known as the **green form**) This is supplied for the funeral director who cannot proceed without it. The certificate is free of charge.
- **A certificate of registration of death** (form BD8) This is used for social security purposes. Relatives are asked to read the details on the reverse of the form and return it to the local social security office if any circumstance applies to the deceased person; for example if they were in receipt of a State Pension or benefit. This certificate is free of charge.
- **A standard death certificate** The Registrar will give you a death certificate only if you ask for one. There is a small charge for this. The certificates are issued for use by banks, building societies, insurance companies and any such organisation that requires official notification. It may be wise to buy additional copies at the time of registration as certificates cost more if you need one later on.

For more information

ⓘ Age Concern Factsheets (see page 197 for details of how to obtain factsheets). Scottish versions are also available:
7 *Making Your Will*
14 *Dealing with Someone's Estate*
22 *Legal Arrangements for Managing Financial Affairs*
27 *Planning For a Funeral.*

ⓘ Department for Work and Pensions booklet D49 *What To Do After a Death in England and Wales: A Guide to What You Must Do and the Help You Can Get* is available from social security offices or local probate registry offices and on the Internet at www.dwp.gov.uk

ℹ Booklet D49S *What To Do After a Death in Scotland*, available from a registration or social security office, or by post from the Scottish Executive Justice Department, Civil Law Division, Room 2W(R), St Andrews House, Regent Road, Edinburgh EH1 3DG. Tel: 0131 244 3581. Website: www.scotland.gov.uk

ℹ Contact the **local probate registry office** (see telephone directory) for information and a leaflet about *How to Obtain Probate* (PA2).

Conclusion

This chapter has covered a wide range of services, available from many organisations and agencies in the private, public and voluntary sectors. If you have read through the chapter briefly, you may find it useful to return to the appropriate section when the time is right, as your relative's circumstances change.

6 Managing stress

Caring for someone who is unwell is stressful for lots of reasons – anxieties about the illness, the extra pressures of caring and the difficulty of managing your own life can all compete with each other to exhaust your mental energies. It's no wonder most carers say that tension rarely sinks far below the surface.

This chapter describes stress in general and helps you to think about some of the personal problems that may be causing your stress. How you deal with difficult situations depends on lots of factors – your personality type, whether you feel in control of the situation, and how much energy you have in reserve, all play their part in how well you cope.

Everyone needs a few strategies to draw on when the going gets tough. This chapter offers some suggestions to help you build up your personal strengths and support systems, and a selection of coping skills and self-help techniques to use when you need to act calmly and reduce the tension. Learning how to relax your body works wonders when you are feeling over-tired and pressured.

What is stress?

Jane

'I was so uptight I felt as if I would burst.'

The word 'stress' is very popular nowadays and is commonly used to describe the way we feel when pressure is intense. It's not a medical problem but a combination of symptoms produced when our physical, mental and emotional systems go into overdrive. Everyone reacts to stress in the same physical way, whatever the cause or size of the problem, because we are all programmed to behave alike. Unfortunately, however, some people seem to get more upset than others when faced by difficult situations. This more extreme reaction to stress is often a result of their emotional state, their personality type and how well they have learned to cope in the past rather than due to the nature of the problem.

The problems may stem from:

- loneliness and isolation;
- shortage of time;
- uncertainty about the future;
- difficult relationships and pressures from other people;
- feeling that life is getting out of control; or
- feeling undervalued, overworked and ill-informed.

Joan

'When the pressures built up, I wasn't surprised when I found I had raised blood pressure.'

Having to cope with a bit of stress is normal and is important to help people deal with challenges in a positive way, but when there are too many pressures the reaction can be unpleasant. As tension builds up the body goes into overdrive and produces high levels of adrenaline hormone to prepare itself for action in the same way as a primitive caveman who needed to fight or run away from danger ('fight or flight'). However, nowadays this type of 'escape' is rarely needed, so, instead of using up the energy generated to deal with the danger (stressful situation), it remains in the body, keeping it in a continual state of tension. While adrenaline levels remain high, the body is constantly in the 'red zone' waiting for the next problem that may lurk around the corner.

When stress becomes distress

A little stress can improve performance: it keeps your brain stimulated and helps you to concentrate and deal with challenging situations. For example, many TV presenters regard a bit of stress as essential: it adds sparkle to their performance and keeps them alert. In everyday terms, you can probably relate this to how you feel as an important event draws near. Your nerves are a bit on edge but your body is designed to deal with the occasional stressful event and after it's over you begin to relax and everything slows down. Unfortunately, if difficult situations happen close together, your body doesn't have sufficient time to recover between the periods of pressure and you begin to feel unwell. The tension can become so intense that you may feel as if you are about to explode and you can no longer handle all of the demands being made of you. Relaxing becomes more difficult as your body tells you that it feels *distressed*.

Mike

'My wife was in hospital; I had to keep my business running and then visit her before I went back to do the paperwork. The thought of the VAT figures filled me with dread.'

Joan

'When my husband was ill and I had my mother to see to as well, I'd have given anything for a day on my own.'

Warning signs

Maureen

'When my mother spilt her tea yet again, I saw red. Why couldn't she be more careful. I was late for work, my boss had asked me twice for a report and I had a splitting headache.'

Joan

'To protect my husband I tried to keep life on an even keel, so I took more stress on my own shoulders.'

The typical signs and symptoms that develop when you are feeling over-stressed are triggered by a combination of physical and emotional reactions. Look at the list below and tick the ones that trouble you regularly. If it's more than a few, the time is right to consider some solutions before your own health begins to suffer. The symptoms include:

- headaches;
- feeling tired and listless;
- difficulty in sleeping at either end of the night;
- palpitations and rapid pulse rate;
- indigestion/heartburn;
- breathing problems;
- aching joints;
- overeating or under-eating;
- skin problems;

- increased urine output and diarrhoea;
- numbness and pins and needles in limbs;
- poor concentration and difficulty making decisions;
- feeling unhappy and depressed;
- feeling angry, frustrated and helpless;
- feeling irritable and tearful;
- feeling anxious and fearful; and
- lost sense of humour.

Where do the stresses come from?

John

'For me the worst part is the tiredness. It makes me irritable and I can't think straight. I long for a break but don't know where to start looking for help. I feel close to collapse.'

Joan

'Peter's illness was always at the back of my mind. When I went out I would always wonder what I might find at home when I returned.'

It is difficult to define stress clearly because it seems to come from two directions, both external and internal. The confusion arises when we talk about stress as a *cause* of problems (pressures from people or situations) or as an *effect* (a response from inside our bodies, such as a tension headache). Both external and internal stresses affect our moods and the physical ability to cope. Unfortunately, not all sources of stress are within our control, and problems can rarely be put into neat little boxes. Mostly we manage to keep the 'lids on the boxes' and give our bodies sufficient rest before dealing with the next set of problems. However, if a string of events happen too close together, pressure builds up to uncomfortable levels and it takes only one small problem to bring everything to a head.

Psychologists refer to these sources of stress as 'life events' and they include major upheavals such as retirement, moving home, changing job, an accident and illness but also lesser events such as Christmas or going on holiday. They aren't particularly special or rare and they aren't necessarily unpleasant, just things that happen to all of us all of the time. Research has shown that, if a combination of events follow hard on each other, without giving the body time to recover, the effects are always worse. The important point to note is that it is the accumulation of both minor and major events that happen close together rather than merely the severity of the events.

Linda

'It was hot and my husband was late, which made me feel even more stressed because I dread facing the supermarket to do a big shop when it gets busy.'

If a pattern of events has caused a build-up of tension, it doesn't take much to set nerves jangling. Common predisposing factors are:

- tiredness caused by insufficient sleep or broken sleep patterns such as waking early;
- prolonged pain, perhaps from aching joints or the continual physical strain of moving an ill person;
- strong emotional feelings that stem from anger, sadness or anxiety;
- personality type – some people tend to be more prone to stress than others, particularly if they are impatient by nature;
- pressures created by people or places – relatives, hospital appointments, shopping in crowded supermarkets;
- discomfort caused by lack of fresh air, too much noise or feeling too hot or too cold;
- the weather – some people are affected by too little sunlight;
- things that affect the digestive system – too much alcohol, caffeine in tea and coffee, or refined sugar;

- smoking too many cigarettes – stress is the reason many people give for their smoking habit but in the long term it works in reverse because nicotine affects tolerance to stress; or
- changes in lifestyle that cause uncertainty, such as giving up work, illness or financial worries.

Two personal stories

Jane and Brenda are typical examples of how stress builds up into distress.

Jane

'My husband and I had recently moved house and I felt unsettled and isolated from my friends. My mother suffered a heart attack that caused a great deal of anxiety. I had to travel a long distance to visit her over several weeks and still felt worried after she was settled back at home because I didn't know how well she was taking care of herself. I couldn't sleep because I was uncertain about the future and began to feel unwell with quite a lot of physical and emotional symptoms – bad headaches, extreme tiredness, poor appetite and feelings of panic. The final straw came when someone drove into the back of my car. I felt all alone and didn't know where to turn for help.'

Brenda

'I had been taking care of my father for six months following an operation, and I was beginning to feel at the end of my tether. Besides looking after him twice a day, I had a number of other pressures that all seemed to be falling on my shoulders. We were short of staff at work, my boss did not like me having time off to take my father to the hospital and my daughter was pregnant. I was very tempted to start smoking again even though I had given up several years ago. The situation came to a head one day when I burst into tears over a minor event which felt like a mountain. When the situation had calmed down I was left feeling drained, trembling and confused at the strength of my own emotions. Fortunately, a good friend persuaded me I needed to ask for help, so I talked to my GP who arranged for me to see a qualified counsellor in the practice. It helped enormously to talk to someone who listened without passing comments.'

Brenda and Jane had each gone through a difficult period in a short time with a run of problems adding to their stress load. Each story illustrates the kinds of factor that characterise the build-up of pressure:

- a series of stressful events close together;
- little control over the individual situations;
- pressure from other people; and
- little time for their own relaxation.

Brenda is lucky to have had a caring friend who recognised the signs of stress and helped her to find a safety valve by talking to a counsellor. Self-help is also an important way to solve problems, and what people learn about themselves while dealing with a difficult situation increases their ability to cope with future stress. Be aware of early warning signs and learn how to recognise your own body signals so that you can reduce the pressure before it builds to uncomfortable levels. However, there are no magic potions – stress management, like any other skill, needs to be learned and practised.

Getting the balance right

The key to managing stress is getting the balancing act right between tension and relaxation – like a juggler, if you get too many balls in the air at once they all come bouncing down. Balancing the needs of your relative against your own needs may not be easy. Caring brings extra responsibilities and you may be the main person they rely on. Unfortunately, you are the one most likely to end up with too much stress and too little time for relaxation. Tension and anxiety can't be switched off to order, but this does not mean they should be ignored.

139

There are ways to ease the pressure and give your body a rest, and stress is easier to bear if you understand where the problems are coming from and you feel that you have some control over how the situation is managed.

Iris

'I divide the day into three parts – morning, afternoon and evening. I take each part at a time and have learned to be flexible, to manage what I can.'

Joan

'When it stopped, I looked back and wondered how I coped – I know that I tried to keep my home and work separate.'

Stress diary

Keeping a stress diary can help to sort out where some of the pressure is coming from. Start the process by making a list of all the things that have bothered you in the last week. Next jot down by the side of each problem how you felt at the time – angry, anxious, irritable, etc. Now cross out things that you chose to do – they may have been difficult, but if you entered into a situation willingly you were less likely to be upset by the effort. Look at the remainder of the problems on your list and ask yourself if they could be the fundamental causes of your anxiety. The reason why many people get angry and upset about some situations and not others is usually linked to their feelings about choice. It's far easier to deal with a problem if you know that you have some control over the event.

Gill

'My husband is ill and needs care. I want to look after him at home for as long as I am able, however difficult. We are very close and I want him at home with me.'

If Gill's decision to care for her husband resulted from external pressures – for example, from other family members – she would be more likely to feel resentful because demands were being placed on her with little opportunity to say 'no'. However, because she has made a personal decision to care for her husband she feels calm about the outcome.

Mental stimulation

> ### Harry
>
> 'I wanted to be at home to take care of my wife after her operation, so the decision to take early retirement was mine, but I did miss the stimulation of the office. I felt much better when I started an evening class at the local college. A neighbour stays with my wife and I am now learning about local history.'

Stress doesn't always arise from intense activity. It's also possible to feel frustrated and unsettled if you are bored. Challenges keep the body and brain stimulated, so being isolated at home or doing the same repetitive jobs day after day can be equally distressful.

It is unrealistic to attempt to choose or control every aspect of your life, but try to maintain a balance between the challenging bits and the relative calm. For example, if time at home is pressured, don't take on extra responsibilities outside the house and make the most of respite opportunities by doing something pleasant and relaxing – it's not the time to take an adventure holiday.

Helping yourself

There are two ways that people commonly deal with stress. The first is a form of self-defence in which they justify something that they know is not true but convince themselves that in the short term it may do some good. They tell themselves that their actions are for the best in the hope that the situation will improve without too much effort. A person who smokes may say 'my smoking helps to reduce my stress' when in truth they know that this is not the case. Unfortunately, pretending only masks problems; it never cures them and they continue to niggle away in the background.

The other way of dealing with stress is much more positive because it focuses on doing something for yourself and puts you back in charge. This form of self-help encourages you to face problems squarely and find ways to change or adapt situations. There will still be problems, because it is impossible to achieve a stress-free life, but in this way you lessen the effects.

Learning to cope with pressure

By now you've probably got a clearer picture about the main causes of your stress and feel ready to make some changes that will help you to cope. Start the process by asking yourself the following questions to identify your strong points:

- How have I dealt with difficult situations in the past?
- What lessons did I learn?
- What's different this time round?
- Who (or what) can I turn to for support?
- Will the problem go away if I don't deal with it?
- Would talking to someone else help?
- Are the problems as bad as I think or has anxiety clouded my common sense?
- What sorts of change do I need to make to help me get along?

Finding long-term solutions

No one ever cured their stress overnight, so don't rush into hasty decisions. Look at each problem separately with four courses of action in mind:

1 Is it necessary to change the situation? This may call for major action, such as your relative moving into a care home. Making a decision of this nature will be extremely upsetting, so don't attempt

to do it alone. But if you are finding it very difficult to cope, it could be the right long-term solution.

2 Can you improve your ability to deal with the situation? Your stress levels might fall quite dramatically if you ease some of the pressure on yourself and your time. A practical solution, such as getting help with the housework, could be the answer.

3 Do you need to change your perception of the situation? Ask yourself if the problem is as bad as you think it is and try to turn some of the threats into challenges. Positive 'self-talk' works well here: tell yourself that you have dealt with difficult situations before and that you have ample reserves of inner strength.

4 Would changing your behaviour help? Doing things through habit is easy, especially if you are feeling upset, but you may have slipped into patterns of behaviour that increase your stress. If you are rushing around frantically, slow down so that your actions become calmer. This gives your brain a less stressed message. Cut down on the amount of coffee and tea you drink; the caffeine they contain stimulates the nervous system, causing irritability and insomnia. Change any routines that are particularly tiring; for example, avoid shopping at the supermarket when you know it will be busy.

Jean

'I take help now, especially with practical things. My husband used to do all the practical jobs, but I am happy that my neighbour will cut the lawn or drive us to the hospital clinic.'

Joan

'Look ahead and prepare yourself. It's easier to deal with problems and keeps your mind at rest if you have a plan worked out.'

Personal resources

Ann

'My husband is older than me and he's not so active now. I felt concerned about leaving him, but I have to get out sometimes or I wouldn't be able to carry on. I went to see a counsellor and she helped me draw up a list of my main strengths and encouraged me to draw on the support of people I trust. It was very reassuring to think about all of my personal resources. I have:

- firm relationships with husband, children, family and friends;
- good physical health;
- a positive mental attitude – I feel confident and good about myself;
- a sense of humour;
- financial security;
- spiritual support; and
- no dependence on smoking, alcohol or drugs.

The counsellor also encouraged me to think about where I could help myself further. I could improve my ability to cope by:

- finding more time for myself and having a relaxing hobby;
- learning to say 'no' sometimes; and
- cutting back on some of the household jobs that are not a high priority.'

Like Ann, you can also identify your strengths and think about where you feel vulnerable. Then talk to someone you trust about what steps you could take to improve the areas where you feel insecure, at least to the point where you feel less anxious.

Brenda

'I've learned not to keep it all bottled up, and I meet with friends regularly. We rarely talk about my worries, but I know I can when I need to, and it helps.'

Joan

'It never crossed my mind that I could ask for counselling. I had enormous help from my sons but I never thought about asking anyone else.'

Finding support

Any support is valuable when you are feeling under pressure, especially the undemanding type that comes from family and friends. Asking for help is not a sign of weakness; it's more an awareness that problems can seldom be solved in isolation. If you need to talk to someone, ask for a listening ear, as friends and relatives may be reluctant to interfere unless they are invited. Once you have given the signal that help would be welcome, you should discuss with the other person how this can be achieved without upsetting your relationship. It's important to agree a few basic rules at the beginning, because the last thing you want is someone marching in and taking over. For example, the person you talk to must respect your need for confidentiality; you may become emotional and let off a 'bit of steam'; and you must feel free to ignore their advice without giving offence.

If talking to a friend or relative is not the best course for you because you would find this uncomfortable or there isn't a suitable person, other options are available:

- **self-help and carers' groups** run by social services, health trusts or at a carers' centre;
- **private counsellors** (ask at your GP practice or the Citizens Advice Bureau for a list of professional counsellors who are trained and registered);
- **religious leaders**;
- **telephone helplines** (eg CarersLine on 0808 808 7777 run by Carers UK); or
- **the Samaritans** (national 24-hour helpline staffed by trained counsellors who offer emotional support to people who are feeling isolated and in despair – 08457 90 90 90 or see the local telephone directory).

145

Breathing habits

Breathing is an unconscious action that you rarely think about, but over the years you may have developed poor breathing habits without realising their significance. When your body is calm, breathing is slow, regular and deep. Your rib cage and diaphragm expand, drawing air into the lungs, which expand to fill the whole of the chest cavity, and the abdomen swells; then the rib cage and diaphragm contract, forcing the air out of the lungs.

When anxiety levels are high, breathing becomes fast, irregular and shallow, and air enters only the top part of the chest cavity. Fast breathing is a natural body defence set off by the primitive force that helps you respond to danger. It enables your body to exchange oxygen and carbon dioxide rapidly. Unfortunately, prolonged anxiety creates a state where the body is continually on 'red alert'. Oxygen is inhaled and carbon dioxide exhaled in excess of your actual needs, leading to an imbalance of gases in your bloodstream. This type of breathing – known as hyperventilation or over-breathing – is quite common; if it remains unchecked, breathing patterns change, leading to breath-holding and deep sighing.

These irregular breathing patterns are part of a cycle that is self-triggering. Increased anxiety sends messages to the brain to prepare it for action: the body goes into panic mode and the fear reactions start up; over-breathing leads to too much oxygen in the system and causes symptoms of dizziness, faintness and tingling in the face and limbs; these feelings are frightening and the brain receives another false message triggered by the fear, and so the process continues. People who have become 'chronic hyperventilators' often experience a long list of physical symptoms that mimic more serious medical conditions, such as chest pains, numbness, muscle spasm and even collapse. Hyperventilation is not a serious condition and can be corrected by practising correct breathing exercises. If you have felt any chest pains, talk to your doctor first, who may be able to recommend someone to help you with breathing therapy.

Ann

'I found that the breathing methods taught at the relaxation group changed the way I felt, and then I became more in control generally.'

Better breathing

Although breathing is normally controlled by the 'involuntary nervous system', it's possible to take control of the process and calm the system down when feelings of panic begin to rise. People who learn to correct poor breathing habits soon notice an improvement in their anxiety state. The following guidelines will help remedy over-breathing and generally reduce tension:

■ As soon as anxiety levels begin to rise, quietly tell yourself to 'calm down'. This sends a positive message to the brain.

■ Slow down all your movements, because rushing around increases agitation and your body responds by producing more adrenaline to deal with the 'threat'.

■ Calm your breathing deliberately and keep an even rhythm with a slight pause between the in and out breaths; imagine a candle in front of your face that flickers gently as you breathe out.

■ Practise calm breathing at different times during the day so that you are aware of the feeling of taking control; it's much easier to recognise the correct pattern when you are not over-anxious.

■ Feel how you breathe by placing one hand on your abdomen and the other on your upper chest – as you breathe in, the lower hand should rise first.

■ If you think that you hyperventilate, get a friend to count your breathing when you are unaware: 10–12 breaths per minute is average. Over-breathers regularly breathe at 15–20 breaths per minute and can reach 30 breaths per minute when feeling very frightened.

■ If you feel faint or dizzy with pins and needles in your limbs as a result of breathing too shallowly, quietly cup your hands over your nose and breathe in and out into your hands. By inhaling carbon dioxide you

147

will swiftly restore the balance of chemicals in the bloodstream. Some doctors recommend a paper bag for this restoring action but that can be rather obvious, whereas people will take little notice of your hands.

■ Avoid wearing tight clothing that constricts your abdomen and restricts your breathing. Let your stomach muscles relax even if it does make you look fatter; women are conditioned to holding in their stomachs to create a better body outline, but this interferes with deep breathing.

Learning to relax

> ### Ann
>
> 'The counsellor suggested a relaxation group. I was reluctant at first, but I found that, although it didn't change the fact that my husband is ill, I coped better with it all.'

If your body is already feeling tired and strained, any movements that increase muscular tension are an extra drain on your energy reserves. So it's worth being as relaxed as possible in all of your movements. Ask a friend to observe your general posture or catch sight of yourself in the mirror or a shop window. Look out for uncomfortable positions and bad habits:

■ head thrusting forward or down with your chin hard on your chest;

■ shoulders hunched and rounded;

■ arms held tightly across your chest or stiffly by your sides with hands clenched;

■ legs crossed and twined together;

■ restless habits, such as tapping your fingers and feet, or hair twisting; or

■ nail biting and teeth clenching.

Deep relaxation is an excellent way to restore energy and boost your spirit but it does need time and space. Merely telling yourself to relax rarely works, especially if you are feeling overwrought. Relaxation requires practice and it helps if you understand how the technique works. It's all about fooling the system and giving out positive signals that your body is at ease. Relaxed muscles send calm messages to the brain in a similar way that control of breathing turns off the false reaction to danger. When there are no threats, your body rests and restores itself ready for the next burst of energy.

Whole body relaxation

This is the most common form of relaxation and produces pleasant results quickly. It's a skill that is easy to learn but, just as you didn't learn to walk in a day, you won't learn to relax in one session. The technique always works if you create the right conditions and allow sufficient time – about 20 minutes for a whole body session. Eventually, you can cut down on the time and recreate the stress-free feeling anywhere as you improve your skill. If you would like to learn to relax with a teacher, ask at your GP surgery; many stress counsellors run individual or group classes.

Step-by-step technique for use at home

1 Find a warm, quiet place and lie on a rug or sit in a well-supported chair. Use a pillow for support if it makes you more comfortable. Reduce outside noises if possible.
2 Wear loose clothing and remove glasses and shoes. Lie on your back or sit upright in a chair with head supported, arms and legs straight and slightly apart.
3 Breathe in and out deeply for three breaths and imagine you are losing tension; then breathe normally.
4 You can close your eyes at this stage or wait until they shut natu-rally. You are going to work on each major muscle group, starting with the feet. (As you tighten and relax the muscles, learn to recog-nise the difference between tension and relaxation. Hold each

constriction for a few seconds and repeat each action with a short break between.)

5 Pull your feet towards your body – hold the tension – release and feel the reduction in tension.

6 Point your toes hard away from your body and feel the tension in your calf muscles – hold – and relax.

7 Next work on your thighs by drawing your legs tightly towards you, knees pointing upwards – hold – drop back to a relaxed position with feet, lower legs and thighs rolled outwards.

8 Tense your buttocks by squeezing them together hard – hold – and relax.

9 Tense your abdomen in the opposite way by pushing it outwards – hold – and then let it flop.

10 Check your legs again and if you have slipped back into a tense position have a second go from step 5. A couple of deep breaths will help at this point. Your lower body should feel heavy, warm and relaxed.

11 Now concentrate on your back. Arch your spine away from the floor or chair – hold – and let go. (**Warning** Leave this one out if you have any back problems.)

12 Now move your shoulders backwards to expand your chest – hold – and relax.

13 Tense your shoulders next by raising your arms and pulling on your shoulders – hold – as you drop your arms, wriggle your shoulders up to your ears – relax with your shoulder blades touching the floor or chair.

14 Now work on your hands and lower arms by making a tight fist – hold – and relax, letting your fingers droop. As you clench your fists for the second time, raise your arms slightly and notice the tension in your forearms – hold – and relax.

15 Move to the upper arms by bringing your hands across your body, close to your chest – hold – relax them to a position on the floor or on your thighs with palms facing upwards.

16 Relax your neck and throat by gently moving your head from side to side (not a circular movement) and then pulling your chin down to your chest – hold – and relax.

17 Next clench your jaw by clamping your teeth together – hold – and let go so that your mouth is slightly open. That tension probably felt familiar, as clenching teeth is a common habit.

18 Now work on your facial muscles. Press your lips together – hold – and relax. Push your tongue hard to the roof of your mouth – hold – and let it drop to the floor of your mouth.

19 Move your eyes inside your closed lids to the four quarters of a circle and then let your eyelids relax.

20 Finally, relax your forehead and scalp. Frown hard and pull your forehead down – hold – and let go so that your face feels floppy.

Your whole body should now feel comfortable and free from tension. Breathe gently and let your mind wander at will. If stressful thoughts irritate you in this relaxed state, think about somewhere pleasant and, as you breathe, repeat in your mind 'peace in and pressure out'. Don't worry if you drop off at this point; eventually you will learn to relax your body without going to sleep, but use this method at night if insomnia is a problem.

Lie quietly with your eyes closed for a few minutes, enjoying the warm feeling; then slowly bring yourself back to the present. Count backwards from five to one, clench your fists tightly, relax and rub your hands together. If you are lying on the floor, roll onto your side; open your eyes with your hands shielding them from the light. Stand up slowly and try to hold on to the relaxed mood when you return to action.

Getting the best from relaxation

Sharing the session with another person is pleasant. You can take turns to read the instructions or make yourselves a tape recording. Listen to music if it helps to calm your mind, and ring the changes by starting at your head and working towards your feet. As you become better at 'switching off', shorten the session and create a relaxed mood by imagining your body is warm and heavy without going through all of the muscle-tightening steps. Use this shortened version as a mini-restorative, particularly when you are away from home in stressful situations – and begin to enjoy your new, confident self.

151

Fact Box

Comments from a stress counsellor:

■ Negative thought patterns can make an illness worse.
■ Social support from family and friends can help to alleviate stress.
■ Relaxation offsets the effects of too much stress.
■ 'Coping' habits such as smoking, drinking and overeating or under-eating make things worse.
■ Illness can be an opportunity to improve one's lifestyle.

Conclusion

Stress is normal in small doses and harmful when it becomes so severe that it feels *distressful*. The warning signs are common to everyone, but some people – perhaps because of personality type or bad past experiences – react to pressure more quickly than others. The key to managing stress is learning to recognise where your pressures are coming from and deciding whether you have a choice about changing the situation or accepting that some situations cannot be controlled. When your body gives off the tell-tale signals that tension is rising, try to calm yourself by slowing your movements, breathing quietly and evenly, and relaxing your muscles. Let your shoulders drop, and unwind all the parts of your body that have become 'twisted' together. Use your support systems and don't feel it's a weakness to ask for help or show signs of emotion. Crying or allowing yourself to tremble are good ways to relieve tension.

The next chapter looks at some complementary treatments that are excellent ways of relieving tension and giving yourself a treat.

For more information

ⓘ **The British Association for Counselling and Psychotherapy** can tell you about counsellors in your area (address on page 178).

ⓘ The 'Family Doctor' series booklet *Understanding Stress* is available from many pharmacies/chemist shops.

ⓘ *Staying Sane: Managing the Stress of Caring*, published by Age Concern Books (see page 194).

ⓘ **The Royal College of Psychiatrists** publishes a range of leaflets for dealing with anxieties, phobias, depression, bereavement and other difficulties (address on page 188).

7 Complementary treatments to help with stress

We live in a world that is so fast and furious, even our most recent ancestors would probably find it difficult to recognise. Few of us are able to escape the pressures, demands and problems that seem always to be increasing, and 'stress' is a word on everybody's lips: stress and stress-related problems cost the NHS millions of pounds a year in treatment. However, as hermit-like seclusion isn't really a practical option, we need to find other more agreeable ways to protect ourselves from the traumas of modern living.

This chapter helps to do that by looking at some of the therapies and treatments that can be used alongside orthodox medicine to treat stress and give a boost to body and spirit. It describes some of the popular complementary treatments – such as aromatherapy, reflexology, homeopathy and meditation – and suggests how you and your relative might benefit. Some can easily be practised at home using basic remedies and techniques but for others it would be advisable to see a qualified practitioner.

What are complementary treatments?

The terms 'alternative therapy' and 'complementary treatment' are used to describe a range of treatments available from practitioners and therapists who work alongside doctors in conventional medicine. Most of these methods aim to treat the whole body and are intended to complement, rather than replace, orthodox medicine. All complementary treatments can be obtained without going to a medically trained doctor but this does not mean that an NHS or private doctor will not or cannot provide some alternative treatments; some doctors are dually trained and, increasingly, some GPs are recommending the benefits of such therapies. Not all therapies are widely available in the UK; ask at your local library or GP practice.

Florence

'My daughter encouraged me to have a weekly treat while my husband was at his physiotherapy session, so I went to an aromatherapist. It was wonderful. My daughter took me the first time because I was nervous but I need not have been; the aromatherapist made me feel special.'

Many popular alternative treatments originated in the East and have been practised there for centuries. They rely on ancient knowledge linked to herbal remedies and traditional practices that are believed to stimulate the body's own healing powers; acupuncture from China and yoga from India are obvious examples. Some of the newer therapies appeal more to Western scientific minds and are gaining in popularity as aids to diagnosis as well as treatment by practitioners of alternative therapies. Two examples are colour therapy, which draws links between certain colours and mental harmony or stress, and iridology, which examines the eyes for clues to hidden disorders.

Many of these treatments are still thought by some to verge on quackery and the people who practise them to be cranks. But this view is changing and information can easily be found in books and magazine articles; products are displayed on supermarket shelves and complementary treatments are increasingly being offered through the NHS. The change in thinking has come about in several ways: people have more open minds and are encouraged to practise self-help; they feel more confident about choosing and using products from the mounting range of 'over-the-counter' remedies; and the attractive 'natural' herb-based goods readily available in high street stores have helped to demystify the image of harmful magic potions.

However, an element of caution must always be exercised when buying and using products that have been purchased over the counter (ie without a prescription). Many contain poisonous ingredients that could be harmful if the dosage is exceeded. Be sure to follow the instructions carefully, and ask your own or your relative's doctor whether the product might have an adverse effect.

Finding a qualified therapist

A word of caution here: any book, however specialist, can give only limited information and can never be a substitute for the advice and treatment provided by experienced, qualified practitioners. Ask for details of reputable, local therapists at your surgery or health centre or contact the national organisations listed at the end of each section. Word of mouth can be a good form of recommendation but do make sure that any therapist you visit is registered to practise with the appropriate national body.

Don't be embarrassed to ask directly about qualifications, as all trained therapists will be pleased to offer reassurance and tell you how to check. Properly trained therapists take a full medical history before prescribing and have learned about the dosage and combinations of herbs, whereas untrained people can only guess and may do harm. There are some ready-made treatments available in health shops, but, before taking any over-the-counter medication, it would be wise to go to the doctor first, so as not to delay diagnosis or effective orthodox treatment. Finally, whichever alternative treatment you choose, it's wise to consult a medical doctor if symptoms persist.

Aromatherapy

Julia, an aromatherapist

'Aromatherapy may be used to induce a deep sense of relaxation and well-being, combating the negative effects of stress and anxiety.'

The ancient art of aromatherapy combines the restorative properties of aromatic plant essences with massage and is an excellent therapy to try if complementary treatments are new to you and your relative. Its gentle methods encourage reduction of stress, and a trained therapist will ask questions first to discover the best treatment for each individual person. The complex essential oils extracted from many plants are introduced into the body where the 'life force' of the plant's essential oil can have a curative effect. Therapists do not claim that the oils heal directly in the sense that a synthetic drug may effect a cure; instead it is believed that the oils encourage the body to use its own natural healing forces from within. The essential oils are absorbed through the skin and pass through the tissues to the bloodstream and so travel around the body. Different oil combinations affect different parts of the body; for example, camomile can help with digestive problems.

Selecting oils

Julia, an aromatherapist

'When buying aromatherapy oils, always choose 'pure essential' oils to ensure good quality. Labels that state 'fragrance' or 'blend' are synthetic and are useful only as mood creators or to scent a room. There are recognised retail outlets in most high streets – try good health food, body care and herbalist shops and the larger supermarkets.'

Essential oils are extracted from plant essences by a special distillation process that changes their chemical composition. They are used in concentrations that are many times stronger than their original plant form, as each individual plant holds only very small quantities of oil. Rose oil is the most expensive to purchase because it takes 20 rose heads to obtain one drop of essential oil.

Essential oils are rarely used undiluted, because they are too powerful to use directly on the skin (and some might be dangerous in pregnancy). They are diluted with a good quality, unrefined or cold-pressed vegetable oil, such as peach or almond oil, which also acts as a lubricant to allow the hands to move freely over the skin. (A refined oil may have been subjected to chemical processing.) To start a basic collection it is advisable to choose about six key oils from the aroma 'families': spicy, earthy, floral, citrus, herbal, pine-like and woody are good examples. You can then select and mix oils according to your mood at the time of massage. To practise aromatherapy effectively you will need to read about the oils in more depth and learn how to massage them into the skin. The following list gives examples of the essential oils an aromatherapist would use:

- **For nervous tension and anxiety**, use cypress, frankincense, sweet marjoram, petitgrain, rose otto, vetiver, ylang-ylang.
- **As an antidepressant**, use grapefruit, lavender, neroli or orange blossom, orange, patchouli.
- **For stimulation**, use basil, black pepper, coriander, peppermint, rosemary.
- **As a balancer, to relax or stimulate**, use bergamot, geranium.
- **To reduce pain**, use bergamot, lavender.
- **To ease coughing**, use lavender, sandalwood.

It is important to be aware of the potency of essential oils and that their use is not advised with people who suffer from certain conditions – in particular, a history of miscarriage, haemophilia or advanced varicose veins, and during a high temperature. Always read the instructions carefully before use or follow the advice of a therapist. Oils should *never* be taken by mouth unless prescribed by a medically qualified doctor.

Methods for use at home

Julia, an aromatherapist

'At the end of a day, try a ten-minute, luxuriant aromatherapy bath, using two drops each of lavender, sandalwood and ylang-ylang pure essential oils, to promote a peaceful and restful night's sleep.'

The soothing oils can be used in other ways to enhance their effect:

- **Vaporisation** creates a very pleasant effect by burning oils in special containers, so that the aroma is inhaled from the air. It is believed that the healing part of the oil is breathed into the body and passes through the membranes of the lungs into the blood system. Fill the bowl with water, add two to four drops of essential oil and place a lighted night-light candle underneath. Pottery containers and blended oils are readily available in many gift shops.
- **Oils blended with other creams** give extra benefit in skin care to reduce dry skin and enrich hand creams.
- **Hand/foot baths** with five drops of blended oils added to the water relax the body and ease aching joints.
- **Use in steam inhalers or droplets on a handkerchief** to bring relief from colds and catarrh.
- **Use as room fresheners** by mixing two drops of essential oil in a cup of cool, boiled water and spray the air using a plant sprayer; or mix a few drops of blended oil with *pot-pourri* or put a few droplets onto a cloth and lay it on a radiator.

Aromatherapy massage

This treatment has little in common with the traditional Swedish massage, which is much more vigorous. The secret of aromatherapy lies in the skill of the therapist choosing the right essential oil to suit the mood of the person and help their specific problem. Oils are chosen from three main groups in order to invigorate the body and improve mental well-being, to help tone and regulate the body functions, and to create a feeling of calm.

159

For more information

ⓘ To obtain a list of qualified practitioners in your area, contact one of the following organisations:
Aromatherapy Consortium (address on page 177)
International Federation of Professional Aromatherapists (address on page 185).

Basic massage

Eddy

'I wasn't sure at first when my wife said "Let me give you a massage" but she had bought some special oils and I felt so much more relaxed after she had finished.'

Therapeutic touch, particularly from Eastern cultures, has always been associated with helping to heal people who are sick and distressed. Massage is now much more widely accepted in Western society and is used by sports people and as a complement to everyday medicine. As a quick energiser, stimulator or salve for aching muscles there is no better treatment. If you feel tired or have a tension headache, it is easy to self-massage using the forehead and neck versions outlined below. Vaporise an essential oil in the room and use soft music to increase the feeling of relaxation and create the right atmosphere.

Jo

'I was offered a simple massage in my private hospital. It was only my shoulders and arms, not my whole body as that would have been too tiring after my operation. I felt really good.'

Simple massage is excellent for reducing muscular tension, because it triggers several body actions: it stimulates the circulation, eases painful muscles and generally creates a feeling of pleasure. Unfortunately, the term 'massage' can conjure up visions of disreputable 'parlours' from the back streets of the world. The massage described here is intended only as a method of relieving stress that can be done by a professional therapist or performed at home. Touch is one of our earliest forms of communication, so use it as a way of helping someone else. Some people find it difficult to touch another person in a non-relationship, non-professional situation, but this form of stress-relieving massage can be used very effectively with relatives and friends.

Giving a massage

Phyllis

'I got a book from the library and read about massage and was so curious about its claims that I treated myself to the real thing. I know enough now to help my husband and family when they are feeling a bit uptight.'

Giving a basic massage requires little training and you cannot do any harm because you are not interfering with body systems in an intrusive sense. Look upon it as a stroking action that soothes the skin and eases tense muscles. Traditional or Swedish massage uses three main actions: stroking, kneading and striking. The first two are the most useful movements for untrained people to use at home. The best places to start are the shoulders, arms and forehead. That way you can provide relief from tension without either of you feeling uncomfortable or embarrassed.

Before you start

There are a few general rules which you and your relative should follow in order to help achieve the greatest benefit from the massage:

- Choose appropriate surroundings and get into comfortable positions, warm and free from external interruptions – a chair in the lounge is fine.
- Remove your jewellery and make sure that your fingernails are short.

- Both of you need to spend a few minutes relaxing before the massage starts, because tension from the giver can transmit to the receiver.
- Warm your hands and rest them on your relative for a short while, to set up contact.
- Choose a pleasant-smelling oil and put it in a warm dish nearby so that you can dip one hand into it without changing the rhythm. You should give firm, even strokes, applying pressure without hurting (forget pictures of greasy, body-pummelling masseurs!). Keep contact with the skin throughout, because the massage should feel like a continuous flowing movement.
- Change the pressure in different areas of the body (ie light over the bony parts and stronger over the muscle). Most people are not firm enough when they first start to massage. Let your relative tell you what feels good.
- Avoid heavy pressure directly over the spine.
- The areas around the upper trunk are most prone to tension: shoulders, arms, neck and forehead.
- Your relative should spend about 20 minutes resting after the massage to maximise the feeling.

Muscle tension

If your relative is particularly tense, you will feel areas of lumpy, 'knotted' muscle. Pay special attention to these taut places by kneading with your thumbs and the heels of your palms and smoothing the surrounding areas. These areas may be tender, so take care and listen to your relative's reactions.

Forehead

1 Your relative sits in a comfortable upright chair with you standing behind.
2 Warm your hands by rubbing them together and lightly coat them with an unrefined base oil or an aromatherapy oil mixture.
3 Place both hands on the centre of your relative's forehead, with fingertips touching, and then use firm, sweeping strokes, repeating

several times. Keep the movement continuous by replacing one hand with the other.

4 Move your hands in two directions: first sweep upwards towards the hairline and then downwards towards the cheek bones.

5 Finish by resting your hands for a few seconds. Ask your relative how they feel, because it is important for both of you that the massage feels right. Your relative will feel relieved and uplifted, and you will probably feel equally soothed.

Neck and shoulders

Method one

1 Your relative sits in a comfortable chair with you standing behind. Clip or tie back long hair if necessary.

2 Apply an oil if you are going to use your hands on bare skin, but the massage can be done over clothing with good effect.

3 Place your hands on your relative's neck, just below the ears, with fingers touching; in a continuous movement, sweep your hands across the shoulders and stop at the tops of the arms.

4 Repeat several times.

5 Finish by resting your hands for a few seconds. Your relative should feel that tension in the neck and shoulders has been swept away.

Method two

1 Your positions are as for method one, but start with your hands at the neck end of the shoulders, palms cupped over the muscle.

2 Keeping your hands in contact with the shoulders, use the flat part of your thumbs to knead (circular pressure) the area at the back of the neck in as wide a sweep as the thumbs can reach. Do *not* place pressure directly over the spine.

3 Do this as long as your relative feels comfortable. (This area can become very knotty with tension and is a good place to self-massage.)

4 If your relative has a tension headache, knead more up towards the base of the skull.

163

Arms

1 Prepare as before and place your relative's arm on a protective towel, palm facing down.
2 Put both of your hands on the back of their *lower* arm and, using a firm movement, glide both hands up to the elbow.
3 Separate your hands and slide them down again, gripping round the arm, and off the end of the hand.
4 Using both hands, knead the back of the forearm, working from wrist to elbow.
5 Repeat the sequence on the upper arm.
6 Next massage the elbow with a circular movement. Use plenty of oil, because this area can be dry and becomes sore if the elbows are regularly rested in bed or on chair arms.
7 Ask your relative to raise their forearm and, using your thumbs, knead the front of the forearm from wrist to elbow. Repeat several times.
8 Finish the arm massage by lightly stroking (feathering movement) from the top of the arm to the fingertips. Repeat several times and then do the other arm.
9 If your relative finds that your massaging the whole arm is tiring, try massaging just the lower arms and hands.

For more information

ⓘ To obtain a list of qualified practitioners of therapeutic massage, contact the **UK College for Complementary Health Care Limited** (address on page 189).

Acupressure

Acupressure is an ancient skill practised in China and Japan for over 3,000 years. It combines massage with the principles of acupuncture (without using needles), and is thought to have been the forerunner of acupuncture. Acupressure is believed to improve the body's healing powers, prevent illness and promote energy. Practitioners work on known pressure points with thumbs, fingertips, palms, elbows, knees and feet to balance the flow of energy called 'chi', which runs through 'meridians' or invisible channels throughout the body. Acupressure relieves the symptoms of many conditions and is best used in conjunction with other natural or orthodox treatments. It is thought to be beneficial with many stress-induced conditions, such as allergies, asthma, back pain, depression, insomnia, migraine and general tension.

Therapists will take a full personal history and then use acupressure points to sedate or stimulate the energy channels. Weekly treatments may be needed to improve a problem, or your relative could just enjoy a regular tone-up to promote well-being. Instructions for 'self-help' acupressure can be taken from a book and practised on yourself or with a partner; however, it is advisable that only minor everyday problems such as headache or common digestive conditions are treated without the expertise of a trained practitioner.

A useful technique to try will help relieve nausea caused by travel sickness or anxiety. This remedy is supported by research at Belfast University's Department of Anaesthesia that has shown that the use of pressure bands (sea bands) worn around the wrists does ease feelings of nausea.

Method

1 Press with the pad of your thumb on the point called 'pericardium 6', about 5cm (2 inches) from the wrist between the tendons. The pressure should be firm enough to cause some discomfort but not pain.
2 Hold for 5–10 minutes. Repeat as often as necessary.

For more information

i To find your nearest practitioner, contact the **Institute for Complementary Medicine** (address on page 185).

Bach flower remedies

These remedies are named after the medical and homeopathic trained doctor who researched the healing power of plants in the 1930s. He believed that the characteristics of disorders, whether physical or psychological, could be treated by a cure drawn from plants, sunlight, spring water and fresh air. In practice the remedies tend to be used to treat symptoms that stem from conditions with a psychological basis. This does not imply that the conditions are imagined, simply that they stem from whole body experiences that affect the mind as well as the body. Good examples are the conditions that cause people to feel worried, depressed, exhausted, irritable and panicky.

People have always made use of medicinal herbs, but the 38 Bach remedies claim to use the essential energy within the plant rather than actual plant material. This healing energy is stored in a preserving liquid that can be bought in a concentrated form known as the 'stock remedy'. The concentrated forms are then diluted by mixing with pure water and an alcohol preservative. It is usual to combine several concentrates to form the required final treatment. Because the action of Bach remedies is mild, they cannot result in unpleasant reactions or side effects, and can be used with all age groups. Although orthodox medicine cannot offer a sound reason for their claimed effects, practitioners believe that, by looking at psychological symptoms, people are encouraged to review other aspects of their behaviour, lifestyle and attitudes, and this self-awareness contributes towards the healing process.

Bach remedies are available at many health shops and through specially trained therapists. They are intended primarily as a self-help form of treatment and it is therefore very easy to understand and prepare the remedies using books. The following list gives suggestions about how the remedies can be used; to treat yourself you need to read about them in more depth:

- **For exhaustion and feeling drained of energy by long-standing problems,** use olive.

- **For the after-effects of accident, shock, fright and grief**, use star of Bethlehem.
- **For apprehension for no known reason**, use aspen.
- **For tension, fear, and uncontrolled and irrational thoughts**, use cherry plum.

Rescue Remedy

Five of the remedies – cherry plum, clematis, impatiens, rock rose, and star of Bethlehem – were combined by Dr Bach into an emergency treatment he called Rescue Remedy. It can be used for a number of problems associated with shock and injury to help create a calm, soothing feeling. It can be bought as liquid or cream preparations for internal or external treatment and can be used on cuts, bites or after a traumatic experience.

For more information

ⓘ To find your nearest trained practitioner and details of publications, tapes and educational material, and a comprehensive book list, contact the **Bach Centre** (address on page 178).

Homeopathy

Homeopathy uses minute amounts of natural substances to enhance the body's own healing power. The practice is centuries old and is widely used as the sole form of treatment or as a complement to orthodox medicine. Practitioners are trained in homeopathic medicine and many also have a general medical qualification. The name 'homeopathy' is derived from two Greek words – 'homoeos' (similar) and 'pathos' (disease). The principle is that the patient is given minute doses of a substance that, in a healthy person, would cause similar signs and symptoms. By creating a similar condition the homeopathic remedy stimulates the body to heal itself. The skill lies in knowing the potency of the substances and matching them to the specific signs and symptoms described by the patient. Treatments are prescribed individually to patients, who usually receive one high-potency dose of the remedy. Occasionally, symptoms may worsen but this is usually a short-term effect: an early stage of the healing process.

The remedies are prepared by repeatedly diluting plant and mineral extracts or substances that cause sensitivity (eg house dust). Unlike herbal medicine, in which only the direct effects of plants are used, homeopathic remedies are designed to treat the whole person, not just the illness, so the person's overall physical and emotional state must be assessed. There are few diseases or conditions for which homeopathy cannot be used, although there may still be the need for orthodox treatments. Homeopathy cannot cure what is irreversible, and if long-term orthodox treatments have suppressed the body's natural powers these may take a while to regenerate. Homeopathy is valuable in treating conditions such as high blood pressure, gout and insomnia, and can be given pre- and post-operatively to enhance healing.

For more information

❶ To find your nearest homeopathic practitioner, contact:
Society of Homeopaths (address on page 188)
Homeopathic Medical Association (address on page 184).

❶ To find your nearest homeopathic doctor, contact the **British Homeopathic Association** (address on page 179).

Reflexology

Keith

'I was very doubtful about letting a therapist touch my feet because they are very sensitive, but she convinced me that she wouldn't tickle. Once I settled down, it didn't really feel uncomfortable and she was able to help my condition.'

Reflexology also complements orthodox medicine and involves massaging reflex areas in the body, found most commonly in the feet and hands, that correspond to all parts of the body. Practitioners believe that healing is encouraged by applying pressure to these points to free blockages in energy pathways. The reflex points are laid out to form a 'map' of the body, the right and left feet reflecting the right and left sides. A reflexologist takes a full history from the person and uses both feet to give whole body treatment. It's an ideal way to boost circulation.

The method has been used for several thousand years and is described in ancient Chinese and Egyptian writings. It does not claim to cure problems but therapists believe that many conditions respond well to reflexology, especially those related to stress, such as migraine, breathing disorders, and circulatory and digestive problems for example.

The practitioner will initially examine the feet for signs of the primary causes of conditions, which may originate from another system of the body, before moving on to precise massage. This involves applying firm pressure with the thumbs to all parts of the feet that correspond to the body areas giving problems. These related areas in the foot feel especially tender when massaged and the level of tenderness indicates the degree of imbalance in the body. The skill of the reflexologist lies in their ability to interpret the tenderness and apply the correct pressure, bearing in mind that some people have more sensitive feet than others. The number of treatments will vary according to the condition and the response. Reflexology is a relaxing therapy that relies on the healing power of touch rather than substances; at the end of each session people usually feel very warm and contented.

For more information

ⓘ To find your nearest practitioner, contact the **Association of Reflexologists** (address on page 178).

Meditation

Jenny

'I thought meditation sounded weird but, once I achieved the feeling of complete relaxation, I realised how calming the effect was on my whole body. My husband relies on me a lot, so I get up early to meditate and have a bit of time to myself.'

Meditation originated in the East and is still used extensively as part of spiritual custom. People who practise meditation claim many benefits, ranging from reduction of stress through to increased mental ability. The capacity to concentrate the mind is an accomplished skill that will be an advantage in other areas of your life, and the relaxed state of mind it brings can help to reduce high blood pressure.

Before starting to meditate it is essential to have learnt to relax by more orthodox methods in order to achieve a tranquil state. The object is to attain a state of complete relaxation in mind and body by focusing thoughts on a single abstract image, article or word. Through this strict discipline the mind can be isolated from everyday worry and fear. Most people are content to reach and maintain this level of tranquillity, though others continue to search for greater spiritual awareness.

There are several types of meditation. Try the ones described here for a sufficient period of time to judge results and opt for the one that feels best. You and your relative can practise meditation together or alone.

The object you chose to concentrate on is not important. It can represent a view of a place with happy memories; a vision of colours; a treasured personal object; a word that has a special meaning; or you can 'listen' mentally to bars of music. The key to success is to switch off all external thoughts and concentrate on the object as a means of shutting out other intrusive thoughts and not to make judgements about what you are visualising. Although heightened 'transcendental' experiences may be your goal, initially you should be content to achieve an increased sense of well-being.

The value of meditation increases the more you practise. Make it a daily activity as a way to relax, or integrate the technique into everyday actions by focusing your senses on one task. A simple action such as washing your hands can have a calming effect if you concentrate enough on it.

Adopting the correct position

Poor posture is closely related to stress and is one of its contributing factors. Very constricted muscles send stress messages to the brain, exacerbating a tense, emotional state, and jangling nerves can push the body into a number of twisted positions. Think of the crossed legs and tightly hunched shoulder positions people adopt when trying to shut out external stress. Posture is important during meditation. The traditional poses include the lotus position from yoga, kneeling as in prayer or standing or sitting erect, but these positions are not vital if you or your relative find them difficult. Instead, choose a comfortable position, keeping the spine straight and try to remain still until you have finished. Achieving total immobility is part of the meditation process, so aching limbs may be an early drawback you will have to overcome.

Enhancing the mood

Set up an aromatherapy burner with a relaxing essential oil or burn a joss stick while meditating, as it helps to create a calming atmosphere. The basis of many joss sticks is frankincense, taken from the resin of a north African tree. It has a warm, balsamic aroma and is highly valued for its effects on the mind and the respiratory tract. Joss sticks can be bought readily in many high street shops and health stores.

Method one: concentration

The most basic and probably oldest type of meditation focuses on a single object. Adopt a sitting position with spine straight, head facing directly forward and eyes looking up towards brows or with eyelids closed. Breathe in a calm rhythm and begin to concentrate your mind in one of the following ways:

- imagine a real object, a favourite picture or flower;
- repeat a silent sound in your mind, or a low-pitched hum known as a *mantra* or incantation;
- concentrate on an abstract thought such as peace or love; or
- concentrate on a part of the body such as the tip of the nose or the imagined back of the skull.

Traditionally a mantra would have had a religious meaning, but this is not necessary for your chosen words. Any thought that focuses your mind will work well. Dwell on this object calmly, push away intrusive thoughts and keep drawing the mind back to the object. Initially, other thoughts will creep in every few seconds, but with discipline the time span can be lengthened until minutes pass without distraction. Ten minutes is ideal but a few minutes are sufficient to restore peace and reduce anxiety. The feeling of relaxation is produced through the mind's repetition of sound or thought. When the meditation is completed, stretch your body and bring it gently back to the everyday world. Practised meditators have been subjected to very strong physical sensations while in deep meditation without showing any effects on their levels of concentration.

Other methods

A number of other similar methods can be used; all of which are variations on the concentration technique:

- **Your corner of heaven** This takes the theme of visiting a happy place a stage further. Because you visit this place often in your meditation, you should be able to step in and out of it at will. If it is a room, you can change the decoration; if it is a garden, you can change the nature of the plants and smell the scents. It creates a safe place for you to enter at times of stress and eases meditation because it uses a range of senses rather than a single focus.
- **Tactile meditation** As the name suggests, this method uses touch. Choose a few pebbles or a set of worry beads and move them from hand to hand. As you move each pebble or bead, feel it and count it. Keep the movement rhythmical and repetitive.

■ **Tratak** With this Indian form of meditation you concentrate on a real lighted candle until your eyes water, then you close your eyes and the image is retained in your mind.

For more information

ⓘ To find your nearest practitioner, contact the **Buddhist Society** (address on page 180).

Visualisation

Jenny

'When my husband could no longer go out for a walk, I would say to him "let's go for a walk together along the cliffs" and we would shut our eyes and walk for miles in our minds. It gave us so much pleasure, we could almost smell the sea.'

Visualisation is a method similar to meditation but it needs much less concentration and is easier to perform. It works well whether it's done alone or with someone else. Therapists use visualisation as a healing exercise to help lift the effects of depression and to create a positive attitude towards life-threatening illnesses; it can have powerful psychological effects. It is believed that visualisation influences the brain centres that control hormone and immune systems and helps to strengthen the healing process.

Using it at home is an excellent way to shut out other stressful thoughts and to mentally take yourself somewhere pleasant. The technique works by creating a sense of contentment and pleasure so that the brain responds to this lack of threat by telling the systems of the body to go into rest rather than alert mode. If you try thinking unpleasant thoughts, you will feel the reverse happen: as you think about a difficult situation, the body immediately responds by rousing itself for action, even though the event is imagined. This action will show you how quickly discomforting thoughts can be subdued by replacing them with happier images. Enjoy these extended forms of relaxation alone or with your relative, and hold on to the sense of pleasure and calm for as long as you can.

First you need to sit or lie comfortably in a quiet place. If you are with a partner, decide whether you want to 'visit' somewhere you both know or one person will take the other on a 'guided' tour using a reading similar to the one below. The guided journey takes five to ten minutes after you have spent some time relaxing.

Guided visualisation

To enjoy the experience, you need to be guided through a journey by another person, who reads from a script or tells a story, or you can use a recorded tape if you are alone. The point of the exercise is to follow a set of visual images through pleasant surroundings to a destination and then slowly retrace your steps back to the real world. If unwelcome thoughts creep in, put them aside and continue with the journey. You can write your own journey – real or fantasy or base it on a painting that you both like. Try the exercise below as an example journey.

Close your eyes. You are sitting in a chair in the garden of a house where you have spent many happy summer holidays. The sun is shining and you are relaxing with a cup of morning coffee and a newspaper. For a while you listen to the sound of the birds and the insects droning in the flowers. You stretch your legs, get up from the chair and walk down the gravel path towards the old gate. The path is winding and is lined by a sweet smelling border of summer flowers.

You open the gate and walk out into a shady lane. The dappled sun is pleasantly warm and you set off on a favourite walk. The lane winds gently down hill and, as you walk along, sounds reach you from across the fields. Children are playing and a skylark is calling. The lane turns a corner and opens quite suddenly to reveal the horizon – in the distance you can just define the line where the hazy blue of the sky meets the darker blue of the sea. Closer to land, the sea is a lighter shade of blue that takes on many tones of green above the sand. The cliffs are high and made of dark granite.

(continued)

This walk is well known to you but it never fails to please. You reach the low stone wall with its tamarisk hedge and pass through the gap to the path along the cliff. Here the breeze catches your hair, the smell of sea is strong and the sound of seagulls audible overhead. You follow the path and make for the headland. Slightly puffed from the wind and the exercise, you sit for a while to watch the sea in its search for continuous motion and marvel yet again at the view.

Rested, you close your eyes briefly to store the vista in your mind. You reach to touch a clump of sea pinks with their wiry stems before standing up to retrace your steps. You return along the cliff path and smell the tamarisk as you slip back into the quiet lane. You walk slowly back up the sandy road until you see the house through the trees. You unlatch the gate and walk back down the garden path to rest again in the wicker chair, with time before lunch to think about the pleasant experience that you will repeat again tomorrow.

It is time to bring the journey to an end, so, in your own time, open your eyes, stretch your limbs and start to think about the present.

Other therapies

There are many other types of alternative therapies that can be used to complement each other and orthodox medicine. You can find out more about them at your local library. They include:

- **Chiropractic** Relieves pain through joint manipulation.
- **Flotation therapy** Relieves stress through floating on very buoyant water in a light- and sound-proofed tank.
- **Herbal medicine** Uses the potent healing properties of plants. Note that these preparations must always be used with caution; like all drugs, they can have unwanted (side) effects.
- **Hypnotherapy** Induces a trance-like state to bring about physical and mental changes.

- **Hydrotherapy** Water treatments to purify and heal the body.
- **Osteopathy** Manipulative therapy used widely in orthodox medicine.
- **T'ai-chi Ch'uan** Meditation in motion.

Conclusion

There is a wide range of complementary therapies available. Many, such as aromatherapy and reflexology, aim to treat the whole body, whilst others, such as osteopathy, are used for more specific problems. You and your relative may be sceptical about whether they work, especially if they rely on less orthodox and 'unseen' methods. No therapist or practitioner of complementary therapies will ever claim to 'cure' a patient or to replace orthodox medicine, but they will strongly support the notion that their treatments can contribute towards the healing process. People who use a qualified practitioner can expect to receive more time for treatment, a whole body approach to their problems, and advice about self-help. If your relative's health is failing, it's well worth considering some of these treatments alongside orthodox medicine, as they can bring tremendous relief from distress and discomfort. However, it is always wise to consult with your own medical doctor first.

For more information

ⓘ *Know Your Complementary Therapies*, published by Age Concern Books (details on page 195).

ⓘ Bookshops and most libraries carry a range of suitable books on most health-related topics, including complementary therapies, or ask the organisations named in each section above for a list of recommended books. It is best to check for an up-to-date book as specific titles are liable to go out of print.

Useful addresses

Advice UK (formerly the Federation of Independent Advice Centres)
12th Floor
New London Bridge House
25 London Bridge Street
London SE1 9ST
Tel: 020 7407 4070
Website: www.adviceuk.org.uk
Promotes the provision of independent advice services in the UK.

Aromatherapy Consortium
PO Box 6522
Desborough
Kettering
Northants NN14 2YX
Tel: 0870 7743477 (10am–2pm, Monday to Friday)
Website: www.aromatherapy-regulation.org.uk
For a list of qualified practitioners in your area.

Association of Charity Officers (incorporating the Occupational Benevolent Funds Alliance)
Unicorn House
Station Close
Potters Bar
Hertfordshire EN6 3JW
Tel: 01707 651777
Website: www.aco.uk.net
Provides information about charities that make grants to individuals in need.

Association of Reflexologists
27 Old Gloucester Street
London WC1N 3XX
Tel: 0870 567 3320
Website: www.aor.org.uk
For names of reflexologists.

Bach Centre
Mount Vernon
Bakers Lane
Sotwell
Wallingford
Oxfordshire OX10 0PZ
Tel: 01491 834678
Website: www.bachcentre.com
For list of trained practitioners and details of publications, tapes and educational material.

British Association for Counselling and Psychotherapy (BACP)
35–37 Albert Street
Rugby
Warwickshire CV21 2SG
Tel: 0870 443 5252
Website: www.bacp.co.uk
For a list of counselling services in your area.

British Cardiac Patients Association
2 Station Road
Swavesey
Cambridge CB4 5QJ
Tel: 01954 202022
Freephone: 0800 479 2800
Website: www.bcpa.co.uk
Offers help and advice to cardiac patients and their families. Has autonomous support groups around the country.

British Heart Foundation
14 Fitzhardinge Street
London W1H 6DH
Tel: 020 7935 0185
Heart information line: 0845 0 70 80 70
Website: www.bhf.org.uk
Aims to play a leading role in the fight against heart disease. Funds research and provides support and information to heart patients and their families through the British Heart Foundation nurses, rehabilitation programmes and support groups. Produces a range of publications, including the Heart Information Series. Many publications can be downloaded from the website.

British Homeopathic Association (incorporating the Homeopathic Trust)
Hahnemann House
29 Park Street West
Luton LU1 3BE
Tel: 0870 444 3950
Website: www.trusthomeopathy.org
For the names of homeopathic practitioners.

British Nursing Association (BNA)
The Colonnades
Beaconsfield Close
Hatfield
Hertfordshire AL10 8YD
Tel: 01707 263544
Website: www.bna.co.uk
Provides care assistants, home helps and qualified nurses to care for people in their own homes.

British Red Cross
9 Grosvenor Crescent
London SW1X 7EJ
Tel: 020 7235 5454 (or look in the telephone directory for a local contact number)
Website: www.redcross.org.uk
For advice about arranging for equipment on loan.

Buddhist Society
58 Ecclestone Square
London SW1V 1PH
Tel: 020 7834 5858
Website: www.thebuddhistsociety.org.uk
For information about practitioners of meditation.

Carers UK
20–25 Glasshouse Yard
London EC1A 4JT
Tel: 020 7490 8818 (admin)
CarersLine: 0808 808 7777 (10am–12noon & 2pm–4pm, Monday to Friday)
Website: www.carersonline.org.uk
Acts as the national voice of carers, raising awareness and providing support and information to all carers. Can put you in touch with other carers and carers' groups in your area.

Charity Search
25 Portview Road
Avonmouth
Bristol BS11 9LD
Tel: 0117 982 4060 (9am–3pm, Monday to Thursday)
Helps link older people with charities that may provide grants to individuals. Applications in writing are preferred.

Chest, Heart and Stroke Scotland
65 North Castle Street
Edinburgh EH2 3LT
Tel: 0131 225 6963
Advice Line: 0845 077 6000 (9am–12.30pm & 1.30pm–4pm, Monday to Friday)
Website: www.chss.org.uk
For information and advice about caring for someone with a heart problem.

Commission for Social Care Inspection (CSCI)
St Nicholas Buildings
St Nicholas Street
Newcastle upon Tyne NE1 1NB
Helpline: 0845 015 0120
Website: www.csci.org.uk
The new independent inspectorate for all social care services in England. Can give you details of your local office.

Community Transport Association UK
Highbank
Halton Street
Hyde
Cheshire SK14 2NY
Tel: 0870 774 3586
Advice Service: 0845 130 6195 (local call rate)
Website: www.communitytransport.com
Services to benefit providers of transport for people with mobility problems.

Continence Foundation
307 Hatton Square
16 Baldwin Gardens
London EC1N 7RJ
Helpline: 0845 3450 165 (9.30am–1pm, Monday to Friday: local call rate)
Website: www.continence-foundation.org.uk
Information and advice and details of how to contact the local continence service.

Counsel and Care
Twyman House
16 Bonny Street
London NW1 9PG
Advice Line: 0845 300 7585 (10am–1pm, Monday to Friday: local call rate)
Website: www.counselandcare.org.uk
Information and advice for older people and carers about remaining at home or about care homes.

181

Crossroads – Caring for Carers
10 Regent Place
Rugby
Warwickshire CV21 2PN
Tel: 0845 450 0350 (local call rate)
Website: www.crossroads.org.uk
For a range of services, including personal and respite care.

Cruse – Bereavement Care
126 Sheen Road
Richmond
Surrey TW9 1UR
Helpline: 0870 167 1677
Website: www.crusebereavementcare.org.uk
For all types of bereavement counselling and a wide range of publications.

Disability Living Allowance Unit
Warbreck House
Warbreck Hill
Blackpool FY2 0YE
Tel: 08457 123 456
Information about exemption from road tax for vehicles used exclusively by or for disabled people.

Disability Living Centres Council
Redbank House
4 St Chad's Street
Manchester M8 8QA
Tel: 0161 834 1044
Website: www.dlcc.org.uk
For the Disability Living Centre nearest you, where you can see aids and equipment.

Disabled Living Foundation
380–384 Harrow Road
London W9 2HU
Tel: 020 7289 6111

Helpline: 0845 130 9177 (10am–1pm, Monday to Friday: local call rate)
Website: www.dlf.org.uk
Information about aids to help cope with a disability.

Disabled Persons Railcard Office
PO Box 1YT
Newcastle upon Tyne NE99 1YT
Helpline: 0191 218 8103
Website: www.railcard.co.uk
For a railcard offering concessionary fares. An application form and booklet called Rail Travel for Disabled Passengers *can be found at most stations or from the address above.*

Disablement Information and Advice Lines (DIAL UK)
St Catherine's
Tickhill Road
Doncaster
South Yorkshire DN4 8QN
Tel: 01302 310123
Website: www.dialuk.org.uk
For your nearest local group, giving information and advice about disability.

Drinkline
Freephone: 0800 917 8282 (9am–11pm, Monday to Friday & 6pm–11pm, weekends)
National alcohol helpline that provides confidential information, help and advice about drinking to anyone, including people worried about some-one else's drinking.

Elderly Accommodation Counsel
3rd Floor
89 Albert Embankment
London SE1 7TP
Helpline: 020 7820 1343
Website: www.housingcare.org and www.eac.org.uk
Computerised information about all forms of accommodation for older peo-ple (including care homes and hospices) and advice on top-up funding.

EXTEND
2 Place Farm
Wheathampstead
Hertfordshire AL4 8SB
Tel: 01582 832760
Website: www.extend.org.uk
*Provides exercise in the form of movement to music for people over 60
years and less able people of all ages. Please send sae.*

HEART UK (formerly Family Heart Association)
7 North Road
Maidenhead
Berkshire SL6 1PE
Tel: 01628 628638
Website: www.heartuk.org.uk
*Information on coronary heart disease and its management, particularly
for people at high risk due to cholesterol.*

Holiday Care Service
7th Floor
Sunley House
4 Bedford Park
Croydon
Surrey CR0 2AP
Tel: 0845 124 9971
Website: holidaycare.org.uk
*Information and advice on holidays, travel facilities and respite care
available for older or disabled people and their carers.*

Homeopathic Medical Association
6 Livingstone Road
Gravesend
Kent DA12 5DZ
Tel: 01474 560336 (10am–1pm & 2pm–4pm, Monday to Friday)
Website: www.the-hma.org
For the names of homeopathic trained doctors.

Hospice Information Service
St Christopher's Hospice
51–59 Lawrie Park Road
London SE26 6DZ
Tel: 0870 903 3903 (9am–5pm, Monday to Friday)
Website: www.hospiceinformation.info
For information about hospices and hospice care.

Independent Healthcare Association
Westminster Tower
3 Albert Embankment
London SE1 7SP
Tel: 020 7793 4620
Website: www.iha.org.uk
For information about finding and paying for care in a care home.

Institute for Complementary Medicine (ICM)
PO Box 194
London SE16 7QZ
Tel: 020 7237 5165 (10am–3pm, Monday to Friday)
Website: www.icmedicine.co.uk
Information and advice about complementary therapy. Please send an sae and state the therapy you are interested in.

International Federation of Professional Aromatherapists
82 Ashby Road
Hinckley
Leicestershire LE10 1SN
Tel: 01455 637987
Website: www.ifparoma.org
For a list of qualified practitioners in your area.

Jewish Care
Stewart Young House
221 Golders Green Road
London NW11 9DQ

Tel: 020 8922 2000
Website: www.jewishcare.org
Social care, personal support and care homes for Jewish people.

Motability
City Gate House
22 Southwark Bridge Road
London SE1 9HB
Tel: 0845 456 4566 (local call rate)
Website: www.motability.co.uk
Advice and help about cars, scooters and wheelchairs for disabled people.

National Association of Councils for Voluntary Service (NACVS)
177 Arundel Street
Sheffield S1 2NU
Tel: 0114 278 6636
Website: www.nacvs.org.uk
Promotes and supports the work of councils for voluntary service. Or look in your telephone directory to see if there is a local CVS.

NHS Direct
Tel: 0845 46 47
Website: www.nhsdirect.nhs.uk
A 24-hour nurse-led helpline providing confidential healthcare advice and information.

Office of Care and Protection (Northern Ireland)
Royal Courts of Justice
Chichester Street
Belfast BT1 3JF
Tel: 028 9023 5111
Website: www.courtsni.gov.uk
If you need to take over the affairs of someone who is mentally incapable in Northern Ireland.

Office of the Public Guardian (OPG)
Hadrian House
Callendar Business Park
Callendar Road
Falkirk FK1 1XR
Tel: 01324 678300
Website: www.publicguardian-scotland.gov.uk
Information on Continuing Power of Attorney in Scotland.

Public Guardianship Office
Archway Tower
2 Junction Road
London N19 5SZ
Tel: 020 7664 7300/7000
Enquiry Line: 0845 330 2900
Website: www.guardianship.gov.uk
If you need to take over the affairs of someone who is mentally incapable (in England and Wales).

Quitline
Tel: 0800 00 22 00 (9am–9pm, every day)
Website: www.quit.org.uk
A freephone helpline that provides confidential and practical advice for people wanting to give up smoking.

RADAR (Royal Association for Disability and Rehabilitation)
12 City Forum
250 City Road
London EC1V 8AF
Tel: 020 7250 3222
Website: www.radar.org.uk
A campaigning organisation run by and for disabled people; runs National Key Scheme for disabled people to have access to locked toilets.

Research Institute for Consumer Affairs (trading as Ricability)
30 Angel Gate
City Road
London EC1V 2PT

Tel: 020 7427 2460
Website: www.ricability.org.uk
Tests and evaluates goods and services for disabled and older people, including ordinary consumer products as well as special aids and equipment.

Royal College of Psychiatrists
17 Belgrave Square
London SW1X 8PG
Tel: 020 7235 2351
Website: www.rcpsych.ac.uk
Publishes a range of leaflets for dealing with anxieties, phobias, depression and bereavement.

The Samaritans
Tel: 08457 90 90 90 (24 hours, every day: local call rate)
or see your local telephone directory
Website: www.samaritans.org.uk
Offers confidential emotional support to any person who is in despair.

Society of Homeopaths
11 Brookfield
Duncan Close
Moulton Park
Northampton NN3 6WL
Tel: 0845 450 6611
Website: www.homeopathy-soh.com
For the names of homeopathic practitioners.

Special Families Home Swap Register
Erme House
Station Road
Plympton
Plymouth PL7 3AU
Tel: 01752 347577
Website: www.mywebpage.net/special-families
Home exchange service for people with a physical disability.

The Stroke Association
Stroke House
240 City Road
London EC1V 2PR
Tel: 020 7566 0330 (admin)
Helpline: 0845 30 33 100 (9am–5pm, Monday to Friday: local call rate)
Website: www.stroke.org.uk
National charity which provides practical support to people who have had strokes and their carers. Offers information and education services around the country.

Tripscope
The Vassall Centre
Gill Avenue
Bristol BS16 2QQ
Helpline: 08457 585 641 (9am–5pm, Monday to Friday: local call rate)
Website: www.tripscope.org.uk
A travel information service for older and disabled people.

UK College for Complementary Health Care Limited
Wembley Centre for Health and Care
Barham House
116 Chaplin Road
Wembley HA0 4UZ
Tel: 020 8795 6178
Website: www.ukcollege.com
For a list of qualified practitioners of therapeutic massage.

United Kingdom Home Care Association (UKHCA)
42b Banstead Road
Carshalton Beeches
Surrey SM5 3NW
Tel: 020 8288 1551
Website: www.ukhca.co.uk
For information about member organisations providing home care in your area.

University of the Third Age (U3A)
National Office
26 Harrison Street
London WC1H 8JW
Tel: 020 7837 8838
Website: www.u3a.org.uk
Daytime study and recreational classes. Send a large sae for further information about classes for older people, or look in the telephone directory for local branch.

Winged Fellowship
12 City Forum
250 City Road
London EC1V 8AF
Tel: 0845 345 1972
Website: www.wft.org.uk
Provides respite care and holidays for physically disabled people, with or without a partner.

About Age Concern

This book is one of a wide range of publications produced by Age Concern England, the National Council on Ageing. Age Concern works on behalf of all older people and believes later life should be fulfilling and enjoyable. For too many this is impossible. As the leading charitable movement in the UK concerned with ageing and older people, Age Concern finds effective ways to change that situation.

Where possible, we enable older people to solve problems themselves, providing as much or as little support as they need. A network of local Age Concerns, supported by many thousands of volunteers, provides community-based services such as lunch clubs, day centres and home visiting.

Nationally, we take a lead role in campaigning, parliamentary work, policy analysis, research, specialist information and advice provision, and publishing. Innovative programmes promote healthier lifestyles and provide older people with opportunities to give the experience of a lifetime back to their communities.

Age Concern is dependent on donations, covenants and legacies.

Age Concern England
1268 London Road
London SW16 4ER
Tel: 020 8765 7200
Fax: 020 8765 7211
Website:
www.ageconcern.org.uk

Age Concern Scotland
113 Rose Street
Edinburgh EH2 3DT
Tel: 0131 220 3345
Fax: 0131 220 2779
Website:
www.ageconcernscotland.org.uk

Age Concern Cymru
4th Floor
1 Cathedral Road
Cardiff CF11 9SD
Tel: 029 2037 1566
Fax: 029 2039 9562
Website: www.accymru.org.uk

Age Concern Northern Ireland
3 Lower Crescent
Belfast BT7 1NR
Tel: 028 9024 5729
Fax: 028 9023 5497
Website: www.ageconcernni.org

Other books in this series

The Carer's Handbook: What to do and who to turn to
Marina Lewycka
£6.99 0-86242-366-X

Choices for the carer of an elderly relative
Marina Lewycka
£6.99 0-86242-375-9

Caring for someone with depression
Toni Battison
£6.99 0-86242-389-9

Caring for someone with cancer
Toni Battison
£6.99 0-86242-382-1

Caring for someone with a sight problem
Marina Lewycka
£6.99 0-86242-381-3

Caring for someone with a hearing loss
Marina Lewycka
£6.99 0-86242-380-5

Caring for someone who is dying
Penny Mares
£6.99 0-86242-370-8

Caring for someone with diabetes
Marina Lewycka
£6.99 0-86242-374-0

Caring for someone with arthritis
Jim Pollard
£6.99 0-86242-373-2

Caring for someone at a distance
Julie Spencer-Cingöz
£6.99 0-86242-367-8

Caring for someone who has had a stroke
Philip Coyne with Penny Mares
£6.99 0-86242-369-4

Caring for someone with an alcohol problem
Mike Ward
£6.99 0-86242-372-4

Caring for someone with dementia
Jane Brotchie
£6.99 0-86242-368-6

Caring for someone with memory loss
Toni Battison
£6.99 0-86242-358-9

Publications from Age Concern Books

Staying Sane: Managing the Stress of Caring

Tanya Arroba and Lesley Bell

The aim of this book is to increase the positive rewards associated with caring and demystify the topic of stress. Complete with case studies and checklists, the book helps carers to develop a clear strategy towards dealing positively with stress.

£14.99 ISBN 0-86242-267-1

Alive and Kicking: The Carer's Guide to Exercises for Older People

Julie Sobczak with Susie Dinan and Piers Simey

Regular activity is essential in helping older people to remain agile and independent. This illustrated book contains a wealth of ideas on topics such as motivating the exerciser, safety issues and medical advice, exercise warm-ups and injury prevention and head to toe chair exercises. The book also provides handy tips and ideas on stretching and relaxation techniques, using props and how to make exercise fun.

£11.99 ISBN 0-86242-289-2

Intimate Relations: Living and Loving in Later Life

Dr Sarah Brewer

This exciting new book answers the questions that many older people have on loving, as well as sexual relations, in later life. There are many ways of sharing a fulfilling and enjoyable love life, and there is no need for age-related health problems to get in the way.

A rewarding sex life is an important part of well-being and a loving relationship – at all stages of adult life. This unique book will be of interest to everyone, whatever their age, health or sexual orientation.

£9.99 ISBN 0-86242-384-8

Their Rights: Advance Directives and Living Wills Explored

Kevin Kendrick and Simon Robinson

For some people, dying can be an undignified and demeaning process that robs them of dignity, choice and individuality. In recent decades, 'living wills' or 'advance directives' have been actively promoted as a means of giving people some pre-emptive choice about medical treatment. This book provides a focused and informative account of the key issues surrounding this debate. Presented in a clear, easy-to-read style, the text is interlaced with case studies to illustrate points and encourage the reader to reflect openly and build up an awareness of other people's needs and values.

£9.99 ISBN 0-86242-244-2

Know Your Complementary Therapies

Eileen Inge Herzberg

Written in clear, jargon-free language, this book provides an introduction to complementary therapies, including acupuncture, herbal medicine, aromatherapy, spiritual healing, homeopathy and osteopathy. Uniquely focusing on complementary therapies and older people, the book helps readers to decide which therapies are best suited to their needs, and where to go for help.

£9.99 ISBN 0-86242-309-0

Your Rights: A Guide to Money Benefits for Older People

Sally West

A highly acclaimed annual guide to the State benefits available to older people. Contains current information on State Pensions, means-tested benefits and disability benefits, among other matters, and provides advice on how to claim.

For further information please telephone 0870 44 22 120

Your Taxes and Savings: A Guide for Older People

Paul Lewis

Explains how the tax system affects older people over retirement age, including how to avoid paying more than necessary. The information about savings and investments covers the wide range of opportunities now available.

For further information please telephone 0870 44 22 120

If you would like to order any of these titles, please write to the address below, enclosing a cheque or money order for the appropriate amount (plus £1.99 p&p for one book; for additional books please add 75p per book up to a maximum of £7.50) made payable to Age Concern England. Credit card orders may be made on 0870 44 22 120. Books can also be ordered online at www.ageconcern.org.uk/shop

Age Concern Books
Units 5 and 6
Industrial Estate
Brecon
Powys LD3 8LA

Bulk order discounts

Age Concern Books is pleased to offer a discount on orders totalling 50 or more copies of the same title. For details, please contact Age Concern Books on 0870 44 22 120.

Customised editions

Age Concern Books is pleased to offer a free 'customisation' service for anyone wishing to purchase 500 or more copies of the same title. This gives you the option to have a unique front cover design featuring your organisation's logo and corporate colours, or adding your logo to the current cover design. You can also insert an additional four pages of text for a small additional fee. Existing clients include many of the biggest names in British industry, retailing and finance, the trades unions, educational establishments, the statutory and voluntary sectors, and welfare associations. For full details, please contact Sue Henning, Age Concern Books, Astral House, 1268 London Road, London SW16 4ER. Fax: 020 8765 7211. Email: hennins@ace.org.uk Visit our website at www.ageconcern.org.uk/shop

Age Concern Information Line/ Factsheets subscription

Age Concern produces more than 45 comprehensive factsheets designed to answer many of the questions older people (or those advising them) may have. These include money and benefits, health, community care, leisure and education, and housing. For up to five free factsheets, telephone: 0800 00 99 66 (7am–7pm, seven days a week, every day of the year). Alternatively you may prefer to write to Age Concern, FREEPOST (SWB 30375), Ashburton, Devon TQ13 7ZZ.

For professionals working with older people, the factsheets are available on an annual subscription service, which includes updates throughout the year. For further details and costs of the subscription, please contact Age Concern at the above address.

Index

We hope that this publication has been useful to you. If so, we would very much like to hear from you. Alternatively, if you feel that we could add or change anything, then please write and tell us, using the following Freepost address: Age Concern, FREEPOST CN1794, London SW16 4BR